# DROPLETS OF LOVE

"Rachel Linnett has written an inspiring account of her journey to peace and self-reconciliation. Unsparingly honest, she recounts both her victories and defeats. The result is an intimate and tender invitation to use Rachel's story in service to a conscious and fulfilling life for the reader. She is practical and supportive. She is precise and generous. Her self-revealing good humor is true support for the reader's own revelations."

**–Gangaji**

"What sets this book apart is Linnett's genuine presence and ability to guide readers in uncovering their inner truth. She does not impose a one-size-fits-all solution, but instead offers loving support for each reader's unique healing path.

For those seeking healing, reassurance, or guidance on their spiritual journey, *Droplets of Love* is a gentle companion, urging us to step out of the shadows of pain and into the radiant light of self-awareness and love. This book is not just a read — it's an invitation to transform and embrace life with an open heart."

**–Melissa Bernstein, Co-founder, Melissa & Doug Toys and Co-founder, Lifelines**

"*Droplets of Love* is a must-read for the post-pandemic world we live in, teaching the importance of pausing, setting boundaries, and the significance of being present. It leaves you with the powerful message to trust yourself and make self-prioritization an essential part of life — something we often forget."

**–Jennifer Marrone, MD, FACOG**

"Linnett shares her journey with warmth and empathy, gently opening our hearts and shifting our perspectives to help us take meaningful steps toward a more fulfilled, peaceful, and happy life. This is a book you will read again and again whenever life presents new challenges."

–Judith Velsinger, Family Law Mediator,
Life Coach and Former Lawyer

"If you find yourself compelled to escape the limitations and blocks you created to cope with a difficult childhood, there are times you may feel lost, alone, and overwhelmed. *Droplets of Love* might just be the 'hot cup of cocoa and a hug' you need to soothe you and help you along the way."

–Joel Young, Creator and Custodian
of Non-Personal Awareness®

"I thoroughly enjoyed reading this book and recommend having it by your side during the path to self-love as a helpful resource to support personal enhancement."

–Dr Emma Bradshaw, CPsychol AFBPsS FHEA,
Counselling Psychologist and Co-author of *Trauma Demystified: A Guide for Students and Practitioners*

"A practical and accessible resource for healing, filled with love and compassion. I recommend it to anyone who has made the essential commitment to free themselves from their painful past."

–Rev. Helen Burke, Spiritual Counselor and Best-selling Author of *Just Tell Them I Love Them*

# DROPLETS OF
# LOVE

## THE ART OF LOVING YOURSELF INTO FREEDOM

## RACHEL LINNETT

THE
SELF
PUBLISHING
AGENCY

Rachel Linnett
Droplets of Love: The Art of Loving Yourself into Freedom
TSPA The Self Publishing Agency, Inc.
Copyright © 2025 by Rachel Linnett
First Edition

Hardcover ISBN  978-1-954233-44-7
Softcover ISBN  978-1-954233-43-0
eBook ISBN  978-1-954233-45-4
Audiobook ISBN  978-1-954233-46-1

Book Design | Tracy Hetherington
Editor | Kathie Lynas
Author Photo | Jessica Linnett
Publishing Management | TSPA The Self Publishing Agency, Inc.

"You are not a drop in the ocean. You are the entire ocean in a drop."

–Rumi

For Jess and Josh,
who taught me how to love unconditionally.

# TABLE OF CONTENTS

# TABLE OF CONTENTS

# NOTE TO READER

If, while reading this book, you need assistance in restoring inner balance and calm, please jump straight to the "Serenity Gems" section at the end of the book, where you'll find self-care suggestions. Be gentle with yourself and tune into your needs, taking appropriate action that feels good to you.

*Disclaimer:*

I'm not a medical professional; I'm not giving you medical advice in any shape or form. You are entirely responsible for your own health and mental well-being. Keep taking any prescribed medications and seek help if you need additional support with what arises as you read this book.

# INTRODUCTION

Those of us who had traumatic or abusive childhoods often regard ourselves as damaged goods. We can feel hopeless about ever being able to live our life without being weighed down by painful emotions and limiting beliefs. The reverberations often affect us into adulthood, making it hard to have healthy relationships and lead joyful, fulfilling lives.

I have walked this path and thrown myself head first into improving my relationship with myself and turning my life around.

Through personal stories, insights, and a smattering of tools here and there, this book takes you on an inspirational journey of healing from childhood trauma and opening into loving yourself. It's not a memoir but a book about transforming your life and setting yourself free.

There are no formal teachings within these pages, and there is no step-by-step process for you to follow to guarantee "success" in the self-love department. At its heart, it's a sharing of what has been valuable to me and the path I have taken, in the hope that it might resonate with you, inspire you, and nudge you along on your journey into healing from your past and changing the trajectory of your life.

Perhaps reading this book will help you accept whatever has happened in your life to date and increase your capacity to experience more *Love*, peace, joy, and harmony on every level of your being.

This book is my authentic and humble *Love* offering to the world — my contribution to the evolution of humanity.

Loving ourselves can be regarded by some as a terrible thing, as if we believe we're better than others in some way. Many of us were brought up being told not to think too highly of ourselves and to always put the needs of others first. In this mindset, comments like, "She thinks a lot of herself" or "Oh him, he loves himself" can be used as a weapon to criticize others. Hands up — I thought similar things in my younger years. Have you ever thought the same thing?

Perhaps what lies at the core of this reaction is the suffering associated with being unable to sense our own light and not loving ourselves. We see this love in another, which annoys us, but maybe it's simply revealing our lack of self-love. Beliefs and feelings about ourselves, like profound unlovability, unworthiness, or self-loathing, can be effective obstacles preventing us from loving ourselves.

Sure, some people fall into the trap of believing themselves to be special because of their physical beauty, status, or money. But I'm not referring to that kind of love in this book. The *Love* I'm talking about is who you are at your core — a droplet of *Love*, an aspect of the Divine.

True self-love is not an egotistical act; I regard it as an essential and beautiful part of caring for ourselves on every level.

Loving ourselves is about nurturing, nourishing, and respecting ourselves, and accepting ourselves just as we are without needing to change a thing. It means living a life with healthy boundaries, listening to ourselves, and forgiving ourselves for everything we have or have not done. In this way, we can let ourselves off the hook and become kinder and more compassionate with ourselves. Connecting with our true essence and opening to loving ourselves radically changes every aspect of our existence.

An intrinsic part of the healing journey from our painful pasts is the willingness to experience the totality of our lives: taking our awareness into the core of our toughest emotions, meeting whatever we discover, without an agenda, while letting go of the story, and falling inside ourselves, being still, and discovering what reveals itself to us.

Throughout this book, you'll hear me mention my guides. Let me explain. In 2006, I heard a loud, confident voice in my head speaking to me about problems I was encountering in my life. It was baffling and alarming initially, but I paid attention to the guidance, began to trust what was shared with me, and started acting on it. Over time, I realized that the voice represented my deeper self, my energetic guides.

Where did the idea for this book come from? About fourteen years ago, my guides informed me that I would write three books in my lifetime. This is the first book.

A couple of years ago, they shared the chapter topics for *Droplets of Love* with me, and the content was written in connection with my beloved guides. They intend that readers who are ready for a shift in their consciousness will receive a transmission from what is contained within these pages. They are on a mission to assist humanity in coming to know themselves as *Love*, and it seems I am a conduit in that process.

Please let go of any expectations of what will happen as you read this book. Let it be fluid, and do your best to be curious about where it will take you and how it will affect you.

Here's a snippet of my history to give you a flavor of *Droplets of Love.*

I had a very unhappy, stressful, and dysfunctional childhood. My parents had a miserable and unhealthy marriage, and explosive arguments were commonplace. My mum left home when I was around ten years old, and I only saw her a few times a year after that. I have one sibling, my brother, John, who is two years older than me. John and I lived with our dad, who scared me, as he was often angry and volatile. He was a self-absorbed, negligent, unloving father, and I repeatedly experienced emotional and mental abuse from him.

My nervous system was hard-wired to a state of high alert, and my heart was tightly closed. I didn't feel safe. Numbing myself was my survival strategy.

My upbringing led me to create plenty of painful beliefs about myself. I deemed myself unlovable and unworthy and didn't respect or honor myself. I felt abandoned, rejected, and all alone.

A big black cloud followed me everywhere I went. I had angry outbursts, didn't trust anyone or let many people get close to me, and when I did, more often than not, they let me down. It was a depleting, rigid, limiting way to live.

I didn't experience sexual or physical abuse or witness

horrific events or actual disasters. It may not have been extreme compared to the experiences of others, but nonetheless, it had a massive impact on every level of my being. Complex trauma resulted from those early years. The long-term trickle effect of neglect, rejection, and abandonment caused a tangled web of complicated, deep-seated issues that plagued my life for decades.

Despite my rough start, I earned an undergraduate degree in Physical Geography and a Master's degree in Engineering Hydrology. After graduating, I worked for an environmental consultancy. I've been married to a wonderful person, James, for over thirty years, and I'm a mother of two gorgeous humans in their mid-to-late twenties. I'm a regular kind of human.

Ironically, until my mid-thirties, I was highly skeptical of alternative healing and spirituality. Clearly, the Universe has a sense of humor, because never in a million years would I have suspected that I would end up on a spiritual journey!

Healing from my painful childhood wounds has been outrageously challenging, particularly in the early years of my journey. I often felt like I'd been dragged through a hedge backward and didn't know how to exist in regular life as a wife or mother. Back then, I would have greatly appreciated a book like this to support, reassure, and inspire me as I dove into healing from my painful past.

I often felt scared, confused, exhausted, and frustrated throughout that time. I didn't know anyone who could relate to what I was experiencing. I was in uncharted territory. I felt very lonely and unsure of what the heck was happening. I sensed there was no going back to the way things were. Quite simply, I didn't fit into that container anymore. My old identity was melting down, and I didn't have a clue who would emerge from the fire. Something inside me was urging me to dive deeper into my connection with the Divine, trust the flow of life, and surrender to *Love*.

This book is for those of you who have experienced difficult, traumatic childhoods and want to break free from old patterns, beliefs, and dense emotions and need some support, encouragement, and inspiration. It's also valuable for those of you on a spiritual path who might be struggling and need some reassurance and guidance. I know how difficult it can be to travel the path of healing from painful experiences in life and how terrifying it can be to face your inner demons.

In writing this book, I'm showing up as a soul friend, guide, and mentor, offering you what would have helped me. Perhaps it will also be a valuable resource to reread when you need reassurance or a nudge.

On so many levels, I'm a different person these days. To be honest, my younger self would barely recognize me. The black cloud has vaporized, and my heart is wide open. I love, value, and respect myself. I have reclaimed my power and cleaned up my boundary issues.

However, please don't assume that I regard myself as a perfect person or 100 percent healed! I'm neither of those things. I have my fair share of personality flaws, and sometimes, I wander off the path, get lost, or trip myself up. But

I know how to get back on track, and I don't let it knock me off balance for too long. While I'm not an awakened being, I'm on a path of awakening. I'm a regular person who happens to have a deep desire to nudge others into loving themselves and to guide them through the ups and downs of their healing journeys.

The truth is, we are an invaluable gift to humanity when we have liberated ourselves from our troubles and suffering.

It requires immense courage and determination to embark on an authentic, spiritual, healing journey. I honor and respect those of you prepared to face what you have most avoided: fear, self-hatred, despair, unlovability, or whatever else is present.

Spiritual paths involve accepting ourselves as the totality of our being: the good, the bad, and the downright ugly. Along the way, we are invited to surrender to *Love*, the source of all that is — getting our egos out of the way and letting *Love* take the lead in the dance of our lives.

Oh, and if your mind has no clue what on earth I'm talking about, that's fine, too! Read on and discover the gems within this book that are meant just for you.

I encourage you to be patient and compassionate with yourself as you travel on your journey. Our healing paths are rarely linear. They are usually meandering and can go around in circles, and we often find ourselves at dead ends or seem to go backward. To boot, things we thought we'd dealt with and evolved through have a habit of returning to bite us on the arse.

I invite you to detach from what you think your journey

into loving yourself will look like or how fast it will happen. In my experience, the most worthwhile paths are frequently tumultuous, and our healing and evolution occur in their own sweet time. There is no rushing the process. Instead, we are called to trust in the wisdom of the Divine and its timing for us.

Along the way, we begin to discover who we are at our core — our true essence that lies underneath the layers of trauma, conditioning, thoughts, emotions, and behaviors. Our light is gradually revealed, *Love* courses through our bodies, and we become available to radiate *Love* into the world around us.

Many years ago, I had a series of private sessions with Joel Young, the creator and custodian of Non-Personal Awareness® (NPA®). At one point, he asked me what I really wanted. I gave the rote answer, "I want to be free." He sniffed at my incongruency and replied, "Come on, what do you really want?" I went inward, and to my surprise, what came out of my mouth with force and powerful certainty was, "I want to know myself as *Love*." As the words surfaced, my whole being lit up, and I felt a massive surge of power inside my body. My soul had spoken.

This fierce prayer to know myself as *Love* has been answered repeatedly. It continues to be my North Star as I navigate life, helping me discern what brings me closer to or further away from what my soul truly desires for this lifetime.

I came to realize that my journey has been about coming home to *Love*. My responses to what happened in my life created sufficient discomfort and pain that I reached a point when I was ready to peel away the layers of conditioning and trauma to reveal my true essence, the eternal aspect of me — *Love* itself. Perhaps you're ready to do the same, or maybe you've already embarked on that journey.

Through my own experiences and those of my clients, I've discovered that one of the most powerful and important parts of a healing journey is developing a loving, trusting relationship with our intuition, our Higher Self, and the Divine. From this connected place, we can love ourselves unconditionally and transform our lives.

I'm here to shout from the rooftops that if I can set myself free from painful experiences and love myself unconditionally, so can you. I know that with every cell in my body.

## A FEW THOUGHTS ABOUT READING THIS BOOK

- Please keep in mind that this book is designed to transition from intense content in the earlier chapters to lighter, more inspirational energy as it progresses. This structure is intended to assist you in moving towards transformation.

- If you feel triggered by what you read and need assistance, please go directly to the "Serenity Gems" section at the back of the book. There, you'll find suggestions and tools to help you calm the storm. If you feel overwhelmed, please reach out to a practitioner or health professional. Don't push yourself too hard — there are no medals for toughing it out. Most importantly, take care of yourself.

- If any inner resistance to meeting your emotions arises as you read, speak to it gently and let it know that it is welcome. The resistant part of you has a positive intention of trying to keep you safe. Thank it for doing its best to take care of you. If you are inclined to do so, ask how you can reassure it or if it needs to relay something important to you. The resistant energy usually relaxes, loosens its grip, or disappears altogether when we reassure it that we are here to accept, support, and love it.

- Take on board the insights, suggestions, and tools that resonate with you, and do your best to explore them with a curious, open mind. Toss over your shoulder anything that doesn't seem like a good fit for you. As you read my words, fresh ideas for your own transformation may come to you. Trust your inner guidance over anything I say to you — enough said.

- I'm not religious, but I am deeply spiritual. You won't find the word God in my book. My words for that energy are the Universe, Grace, or the Divine, and I use them interchangeably.

- Throughout this book, I use "*Love*" when referring to the powerful, omnipresent energy of the Divine or pure consciousness — for example, "to know myself as *Love*"— and "love" when referring to the human emotion, as in "I love mint-chocolate chip ice cream."

- To improve clarity, I use italics for depicting inner talk, beliefs, and thoughts throughout this book.

- I am eternally grateful to my spiritual teacher, Gangaji, for the role she has played in my journey since 2010. Her teachings may or may not resonate with you. In this book, I am sharing my personal interpretations of her teachings and how they have impacted me. They are not necessarily how others have absorbed her teachings. I am not representing her or her teachings.

- Having a spiritual teacher isn't everyone's cup of tea, and it certainly isn't a necessity. But if it calls to you and feels true, pray to the Universe to guide you to your teacher.

- I regard myself as a transformational coach and a spiritual guide rather than a spiritual teacher. I'm a conduit for Divine energy, a catalyst enabling others to change their lives. I'm more than happy to leave spiritual teachings to Gangaji and her peers.

- My personal stories are shared with you so that perhaps you can discover yourself in some shape or form within them. Notice what elicits a response in you and what my words evoke. Focus on what grabs your attention, have a go with the resonant tools on offer, keep an open mind, and lean into the possibility of transformation.

Always remember that I walk this path with you, and I send you *Love* and wish you well as you navigate your way through this lifetime.

# PROLOGUE

In my mid-thirties, I had an explosive argument with my best friend. She said some upsetting things about my marriage that crossed the line for me, and I lost my shit with her, big time. I screamed and shouted at the top of my voice. There was so much fury and anger pouring out of every cell of my being because she'd verbally attacked something so precious to me. I lashed out with my words, and I wanted to punish her by wounding her right back. It was an off-the-scale outburst to someone I deeply cared about. As I screamed at her, I could see how shocked she looked, as though she'd never been treated so badly in her entire life, and that didn't stop me. She left, and that was the end of our friendship.

It had much wider ramifications than a big argument between friends. Our young daughters were best friends, and that relationship ended too, as my ex-best friend refused to let the girls meet up. We were part of a close-knit group of friends, and that was irrevocably splintered and in disarray. It was awkward and difficult for many reasons, and even though I knew what she'd said had crossed a line, I grieved the loss of my best friend.

This incredibly upsetting incident was my wake-up call, representing a turning point in my life. Deep down inside, I knew that I had to do something about my anger issues; it wasn't okay to unleash my rage on others. I'd had a traumatic childhood; I'd bottled it all up inside, and I needed help. It was time to heal myself.

The Universe responded to my call for help by sending a remarkable person my way. Around that time, I became great friends with Alison, an intriguing, soulful being. Our friendship changed my life and set me on my healing path, and I'm eternally grateful to her for being such a powerful catalyst of transformation.

We used to walk together for hours through fields of crops in the English countryside, following ancient footpaths. She talked about energy healing and the nature of reality. I was transfixed; something deep inside me was listening intently to her every word.

She'd healed from a shoulder injury through Reiki. I was skeptical about alternative healing back then. With a scientific background, I was firmly entrenched in my logical brain, but because Alison was a successful dentist, I trusted what she told me. I knew she was extremely intelligent and well-educated, so if she thought there was something to all of this, then I wanted to know more. Intrigued by her astonishing results from Reiki, I asked her to give me my first-ever energy-healing session. Thankfully, she said "yes."

In her dining room, I lay on the massage table, fully clothed. My eyes were closed, and as she gently and lovingly placed her hands on my head, I began to see a fantastic array of bright colors. A huge eye appeared in my mind's eye. It was just looking at me, blinking now and then. As the session continued and she moved around my body, I saw an image of my ribcage opening up, and a stream of black smoke leaving my body. Tears poured out of my eyes — floods and floods of tears. I sensed that they were related to my childhood experiences, that the floodgates had opened so that my healing could begin. It felt as though the emotional weight of my younger years was finally beginning to be released.

Later that year, I became very unwell with a nasty virus and struggled to breathe. My doctor diagnosed asthma and told me I had to take medications for the rest of my life. I heard a voice inside of me telling me not to believe him and to have Reiki sessions with Alison's Reiki teacher. I listened to that guidance and booked a series of appointments with him. During my first session, I felt a tremendous, overwhelming, suffocating weight on my chest, as if an elephant had sat on me. I felt as though I was being pinned down and couldn't move if I tried. I was panicking, but I heard a voice inside of me urging me to stay calm, be still, and let the healing commence. To my utter amazement, after just three sessions, all my symptoms completely disappeared.

I was flabbergasted and returned to my doctor to get checked out. The breathing capacity tests showed everything was back to normal. I stopped my medications, and I haven't had any respiratory issues since. I was so intrigued by this healing that I signed up for Reiki classes to learn the healing modality for myself. That's how my spiritual journey began, right before I moved to America in 2006.

Sharing my story with you is an intensely vulnerable act, one that I haven't taken lightly. Throughout this book, all masks are off; I'm showing up authentically and honestly because I know it will facilitate deeper transformations in you, the reader, when I go for gold. My miserable and difficult childhood, the fierce argument with my best friend, together with my conversations with Alison and those Reiki sessions, were the very things that set me on my healing path, and they set the scene for what is contained within these pages.

This book is about my journey of healing from my troubled past, forgiving myself and others, opening my heart, and stepping into genuinely loving myself. For sure, it can be a challenging path to take, but hand on heart, I know without any doubt that you can do it too. It's absolutely possible.

# PART 1

# Melting

# 1

# ACCEPTANCE OPENS THE DOOR

There we were, just the two of us, John and I, as young kids, huddled together as we sat on the carpet in the lounge; I felt comforted by the warmth of his body, not knowing what else to do, while a war raged on in the kitchen. Mum and Dad were fighting again, screaming and shouting at the top of their lungs, sounding as if they were going to murder each other.

Overwhelming fear, aggression, and blind fury flooded our home. The sound of their escalating voices and the surge of their emotions penetrated every part of my being. As a sensitive empath, I internalized it all; my nervous system was overloaded. It was genuinely terrifying, and my way of getting through it was to shut down emotionally, sitting it out, waiting for them to calm down, and for some form of dysfunctional, wretched normality to return.

My sensitive younger self regularly witnessed these traumatic and damaging events between my warring parents. My mum regarded my dad as the authority figure, and she was scared of his explosive temper. When she felt she'd done something wrong in his eyes, she'd run through her habitual response of extreme panic, self-hatred, and dread.

I remember one blustery day when the wind swirled around the neighborhood, shaking the leaves on the trees. I was very young and at home with Mum. She'd left the front door open while she nipped out front to attend to something. Suddenly, the door was caught by a strong gust of wind. It swung violently and slammed shut, and the tall glass pane that ran from the top to the bottom of the door shattered into millions of pieces in the entranceway and into the hallway. The sharp fragments flew out in all directions. Tiny shards of glass littered the floor, glittering as they caught the light — beauty in the destruction.

I heard my mum repeatedly telling herself how stupid she was. Her self-hatred, mixed with panic, fear, and anguish, was contagious. I was too young to fend it off; her intense emotions filled my body and swept through me in waves, leaving me distraught and horrified. Crouched down on the stairs, on the short run before it turned the corner for the long ascent, I watched her unravel. I felt helpless and powerless, frozen to the spot and unable to move as I witnessed my mum's response unfolding before my eyes. She was absolutely terrified of what Dad would say and how he would respond when he returned from work.

Looking back to those days, I recognize that I had a turbulent and traumatic childhood. I don't have any memories of my parents being happy together. Instead, I remember they argued fiercely and regularly, creating a lot of distress for my brother and me. During a particular fight, I walked into the kitchen and saw my mum brandishing a large kitchen knife at my dad. It was a miserable upbringing in an exceptionally stressful environment, and I spent the first part of my life walking on eggshells, trying to prevent being a contributing factor to one of Dad's volatile outbreaks.

With all this unhealthy and turbulent behavior going on in my family, I protected myself as much as I could by zoning out. I became an expert at disconnecting myself from my feelings, entering another bubble of reality and leaving the traumatic one behind. I wasn't willing or even able to let myself feel the extent of my painful emotions. I found friendships difficult, and I didn't have much interest in having close friends. I did have a smattering of friends, but I preferred to keep myself to myself. I didn't reach out to any other adults for help; I didn't discuss it with anyone, and it felt like my shameful secret.

My mum left when I was around ten years old. She went to live with her boyfriend, a six-hour drive away, leaving my brother and me with our dad, who was an angry, stressed, selfish man who had little interest in being a parent. We only saw her a few times a year after that.

Like my mum, I didn't feel safe around my dad. He had a horrible temper, and I habitually kept one eye open, scanning for potential danger. My body responded to the ongoing potential threat of abuse with an anxious, unsettled feeling that became my norm. My survival mode was active most of the time, and I found it hard to switch it off and relax. I grew up feeling neglected, dismissed, unworthy, and unlovable, as if I didn't matter. My dad often told me I was no good and I'd never amount to anything.

Although fiercely independent and a survivor through

and through, my coping strategies had come at a substantial personal cost. I walked through life with a big black cloud of unresolved issues swirling above my head. I had a stack of awful beliefs about myself; my heart was firmly closed; disconnecting from my troubles through dissociation was a familiar friend; and I had substantial anger and aggression issues. I didn't trust anyone.

Growing up in that craziness, I developed a survival strategy of attempting to manipulate and control situations to get what I wanted, to stay safe, and be loved. I've since realized that we can't control most things in life, and our attempts to do so tend to generate massive amounts of anger, frustration, fear, and vulnerability. When we attempt to control others, they find it intolerable; it's suffocating. I've definitely learned the hard way that you can't make people love you.

We can't accept and surrender anything when firmly entrenched in the need to control. To the controlling mind, accepting and surrendering are signs of weakness or failure, and they're to be avoided at all costs to prevent annihilation. The mind can fight long and hard to retain control, even when it causes extreme misery in our lives. Deep-rooted fears that are often unconscious to us tend to drive this necessity for control. To the egoic personality, trying to control life is a matter of life and death, and it's determined to survive at all costs by avoiding perceived weakness and vulnerability. It takes a lot of courage to meet and embrace our need to control, and the resistance can seem immovable, as if set in concrete.

However, in order to dismantle these control strategies and free ourselves from their stubborn grip, it's beneficial to take ourselves right into the center of the energy field of our desire to control, breathing deeply, not moving, and welcoming it all.

At the core of my control strategies was a lack of trust, a belief that I couldn't trust anyone else to do things properly, so I had to do it all by myself. I also believed that no one else looked after me or kept an eye out for me, that I was in this life all alone, so I had to take control and make sure I got it right. It was up to me to take care of myself.

It was an intoxicating mix that created considerable rigidity in my response to many things that arose in my life, and I became an over-protective mummy bear with my children. It's been tough to shift this controlling pattern, but thankfully, my white-knuckle death grip on control has loosened, and I've become more accepting, flexible, and fluid. I have a greater capacity to accept what is, trusting the flow of life a greater percentage of the time, and letting *Love* take the lead — rather than needing to force, drive, and control things into being.

Uncovering my control strategies has been an integral part of my healing journey, and it continues to be an ongoing practice for me, as it reappears regularly. I notice it most when I sense things aren't going to plan, and it feels like I'm paddling upstream in a canoe with holes in it. Then, with honesty, I can take an objective look to see if I'm trying to force things into being, to determine if I'm attempting to make something work the way I desperately want it to. If I sniff control, that's my cue to pause, take some deep breaths, and open to the controlling energy inside me, which always leads me to a humble and loving place of acceptance and surrender. When I'm deeply entrenched in my thoughts, most often when I'm feeling very stressed or overwhelmed, it can take quite a while to recognize that's what's happening. But the moment I'm aware of its presence, it's simply an opportunity to go inwards, be gentle and loving towards myself, and embrace the urge to control — and then it tends to fall away with relative ease.

I've learned from direct experience that when we don't accept the difficult things that happen in our lives, we suffer, and the more we wish things were different, the worse that suffering gets. When we accept, love, and embrace painful experiences and the emotions that arise, we can heal our past, turn our lives around, and open up to a deeper capacity for loving ourselves. It really is that simple, but despite the simplicity, it can be extremely challenging to accept the tough stuff that roars through our lives.

Sometimes I think that it's a miracle I survived my teenage years and healed from my childhood wounds. I was only able to fully accept my past after I'd cleared out my perceived unlovability and unworthiness, softened my rigidity, and released a potent cocktail of painful emotions that were locked up inside of my body. Over time, I peeled away layer upon layer of hurt, shame, fear, guilt, sadness, and anger, and the more I released, the better I felt.

I believe that the Divine has a plan for each of us. Perhaps it's our soul's purpose for this lifetime, so that we experience certain events and relationships to give us an opportunity to grow and evolve as souls, if we so choose. Our job is to get out of the way and let our hearts take the lead rather than believing we can make anything happen through force, manipulation, and willpower. In my experience, the key lies in giving ourselves permission to surrender to the Universe, to *Love*, to open up on every level of our being and trust that something much bigger and more powerful is at play than our human minds can comprehend.

My arrival in America marked the beginning of a dark night of the soul for me. "Sorry folks, we won't be landing at JFK as scheduled. They've closed the airport because of the winter storm, so we're flying to Washington, DC." On February 12, 2006, my husband, James, and I, along with our kids Jess, aged 9, and Josh, 6, were on our way to America, emigrating from England. It was stressful enough without the unwelcome addition of a dangerous snowstorm. I was leaving behind everything I'd ever known: my dearest friends, my family, my beautiful homeland, and a deep familiarity with how life operated in the UK. Oh, and let's not forget Marks & Spencer food halls; that one would hurt, too!

We landed on the runway in DC, sat on the plane for a few hours, and were not allowed to disembark. Finally, the courageous captain informed us that he would have a go at getting into JFK as the airport had re-opened. We flew back up to New York City and were the second-to-last plane to land that night; the one after us skidded off the runway in treacherous conditions.

It was certainly a dramatic way to enter the country that would become our new home. We'd rented an enormous Yukon XL truck from the car-rental company, as we had so much luggage; neither James nor I had ever seen such a massive truck. We came from the land of small cars, and it felt like a tank compared to what we'd driven before!

We drove slowly and carefully from JFK to Madison, New Jersey, our new hometown. The snow fell as hard as icing sugar through a sieve, and it was tough to see where we were going. The highways hadn't been cleared properly, and we had to navigate deep snow on the local roads. We'd never seen anything like it; we looked in amazement and trepidation at cars in the forecourt of the Honda dealership on Main Street, with several feet of snow piled on top of them. That was the first time I'd laid eyes on Madison.

I hadn't wanted to move to America. The timing was rough for me, as I'd just qualified as a Pilates instructor after an intensive year of studying and supervised teaching. I'd planned to become trained as a physiotherapist so that I could offer both physical therapy and Pilates to assist people with injuries and health issues. After all those years of staying home with the kids, I'd finally stepped up and done something for myself. I was genuinely passionate about offering these services to people. However, an excellent promotion opportunity came up for James in New York City, which was hard to refuse and would potentially change his career, so after many discussions, we decided to move our family to America.

I struggled to integrate into the American way of life in small-town New Jersey. I felt like an outsider and sorely needed an "idiot's guide" to living in America as a Brit. It took me three months to discover that you could put your mail in the mailbox at the end of the driveway, and the mailman would take it away! I struggled with the way banks worked and how to deal with the Post Office. I spent hours in supermarkets clueless about brands, all of it unfamiliar, and not knowing what was good and what wasn't — finding a brand of wholemeal bread with no added sugar took a while too. I had so many questions to ask people about how things worked and what they recommended for all kinds of things that I needed to run our family life that I had to dish them out to different people so that I didn't overload one person. Getting the simple things done was overwhelming and took a lot longer than I had the patience for. It was exhausting.

I was clueless about the kids' sports like baseball, lacrosse, and cheerleading. I was concerned when I found out that from time to time, hungry black bears roamed the streets of our town, raiding bird feeders for food. The police alerted town residents when a bear had been spotted in the neighborhood to ensure we stayed safe. I was unnerved when I encountered snakes on the trails through the Loantaka Brook Reservation, where I walked the dog and rode my bike. People even drove differently in the Tri-State area compared to the UK. It felt like utter chaos, with no lane discipline and people weaving in and out of traffic, traveling way over the speed limit — a far cry from the orderly driving in the UK.

I missed my friends; I had no one to tell how lonely and isolated I felt. I had no one to go and have a couple of glasses of wine with and a good laugh about everything I was experiencing. I was reluctant to share with the locals what I found so bizarre about American culture, as I was concerned that if I did, it would be construed as criticism and make it even harder for me to settle in and make friends. So, I became very good at wearing masks, feeling thoroughly miserable while putting on a smiling face.

It was tough for my kids too. They were finding their way in school, while sorely missing their friends back home and struggling to make new ones. They were figuring out how to fit into an alien culture, and to make matters even harder for them, the elementary school put them both up a grade beyond their age group within a week of our arrival, deeply troubling me as their mum. For social and developmental reasons, I firmly believed it was in their best interest to stay with their own age group. Having started full-time school at four years old in England, they were more advanced than their American peers. I felt stuck between a rock and a hard place, not knowing the best thing for them — to be in the most appropriate grade for their academic development or the best grade for their social development. I felt so guilty that I'd done this to them; they'd been in an excellent school system in England. But the school was adamant they couldn't cater to them in their proper age group.

James worked long hours, and I barely saw him on weekdays. He loved being in America; he embraced it all. But me? I'd have gone home to the UK in a heartbeat. I struggled to tread water, and I felt like I was barely getting enough air inside of me when I rose to the water's surface, gasping for oxygen. I was too upset even to call my friends back home. I knew that it would just make me feel worse. Going home wasn't an option; it was a permanent move, not a secondment.

For many years, I resented and blamed James for my predicament, even though I'd agreed to move. I felt desperately lonely and unhappy, and I fiercely resisted living here. A couple of health issues started up within months of my arrival, and I'm convinced that an emotional component had contributed to their emergence, fueled by my lack of resonance with America, feeling powerless about my situation, and grieving my homeland. The truth is I could have spoken up and insisted that we move back home, but I couldn't find my voice to do that. I believed that I didn't have a choice in the matter, that I had to be the dutiful wife and support James and his career, regardless of how miserable I was.

It took me years to address my resentment and blame towards James for us living in America. I finally saw that I was the one creating my suffering from my repeating thoughts of blame, powerlessness, and resistance. My intense emotions propelled me onto my spiritual journey; they were the perfect storm for massive personal transformation. Leaving my homeland gave me a fabulous opportunity to accept my troubled childhood. It was the uncontrollable pain that forced me to take action, being so far from home and feeling completely alone and isolated, with no one to comfort me.

We haven't a clue what our journey through life will be; bizarrely, our toughest challenges often turn out to be central to our self-discovery — the very thing we most need in our personal evolution.

As a curious being who loves to learn, I became trained in numerous energy-healing modalities and continued delving into healing the buried wounds from my childhood. I opened into accepting my past and surrendering to the wisdom of the Divine for bringing me here. A bigger force was at work, planting me in America.

As time went by, I made some wonderful friends in Madison who helped me to navigate life in New Jersey. They laughed at my English ways and were charmed by my accent. Since moving to America, I've had countless amazing experiences, met so many incredible people, and continue to do so — including those who became dear friends, those who made me laugh out loud, and those who inspired me. Some treated me with immense unkindness and a lack of respect, and they became my greatest teachers. Their behavior showed me what I had overlooked in my psyche, where I was treating people poorly and wasn't being kind to myself or respecting myself, a far cry from self-love. With these deeply hidden parts of me made conscious, I was able to take important steps forward into loving myself.

On reading this chapter, you may have seen some similarities with your own life, or perhaps, although different from your experiences, it reminded you of some of your most challenging times. With tenderness and compassion, keeping an open mind, I invite you to lean into what's arising for you as you read my words — setting aside some quiet time for yourself to pause for a while to discover what patterns, emotions, or beliefs may have been triggered. We may have some energetic threads in common. Were there events in your childhood that created tremendous suffering for you? If so, how has that history impacted your life, and is it still doing so today? Has it affected how you feel about yourself or how you're able to love yourself? Please do your best to be honest and gentle with yourself as you sit with this, and I encourage you to let go of any judgment or negative self-talk while you investigate what lies inside of you that's calling for healing and resolution.

I'm about to guide you through a short, simple exercise designed to help you accept something challenging in your life, supporting you on your journey into self-love.

Wherever you are on your healing journey, at the beginning or at any point along the path, I invite you to pause for a moment and listen to your heart, and if it resonates, take yourself inside with gentleness and a loving embrace.

Open your awareness in all directions, in front of you, behind you, beneath you, above you, and to all sides. Be still in the resulting spaciousness and ask to be shown something you need to accept in your life. Then, be patient and see what bubbles up inside. You may recall specific events, or you may feel some uncomfortable or painful emotions — like anger, fear, or sadness — or it could show up in any number of other ways.

In whatever way it arises, meet the places where resistance and non-acceptance exist inside of you. Withdraw your attention from any thoughts that may appear about your personal history or who did what to whom. In this moment, refuse to be lured by your thoughts, regardless of how convincing or loud they may seem. The mind can be very persuasive and tenacious, but do your best to let go of your thoughts and narrative.

Breathe deeply and say "yes" to acceptance and surrender, discovering where that takes you. Breathe in acceptance to the places that are tight, tense, or calling out to you, and breathe out whatever emotions are ready to leave your energetic system. Sometimes, your emotions may feel more intense as you do this; if so, please know it's all okay. Welcome any increased intensity and relax anywhere that feels tight inside your body. Just focus on breathing in acceptance and breathing out whatever no longer serves you. Continue until you feel complete, and trust that you'll know when it is done for today. It's quite likely at this point, you'll be experiencing a sense of calmness or spaciousness inside of you, to a greater or lesser degree.

In this peaceful, expansive place, ask to be shown how to accept the situation fully. Is there something you need to know about what has occurred, or are there are any actions you can take to support and love yourself? Keep breathing gently, deeply, slowly, and fully. You may wish to make a note of anything that comes to you, as it can be easy to forget when the moment has passed.

When you feel complete, take a moment to return to full wakefulness. Wriggle your fingers and toes and notice the temperature of the air on your face. Afterward, drink plenty of water, and if possible, take a bath with magnesium flakes or Epsom salts to help with the release process. It's important to honor and love yourself by following through on any actions you feel guided to take. This will deepen your ability to trust your inner wisdom and strengthen your relationship with your inner self.

The journey into loving ourselves becomes smoother when we open ourselves to accepting difficult moments from our past, freeing ourselves from painful patterns and experiences that have troubled us. Acceptance and surrender are powerful allies in facilitating potent and lasting transformations, making it easier to love ourselves. As our self-love deepens, every aspect of our lives improves.

# 2

# STANDING STILL IN
# THE INFERNO

It's extremely common to struggle with deep-rooted fears of intimacy, loneliness, or being abandoned when we've endured abusive, painful childhoods. When we've been traumatized, abandoned, or rejected, we may become terrified of it happening again. In response to these fears, unhealthy behaviors and attitudes frequently arise that have a nasty habit of creating further problems for us, limiting our ability to have healthy relationships and live wonderful lives.

The fear of abandonment was a persistent, pervasive, and powerful force in my life for many years.

At the time of my birth, my mum wasn't feeling well. The hospital staff were concerned that she might have the flu. So, immediately after my birth, I was separated from her and placed in a baby unit to keep me free from infection. For the first ten days of my life, I didn't experience loving maternal hugs, kisses, smells, or body warmth to soothe and reassure me. It was an unfortunate situation where everyone was doing the best they could to keep me healthy.

A sense of abandonment returned when my mum left home. I don't remember the actual moment she left or how old I was, although I think I was around ten. Only one memory remains from that highly emotional time. Mum and I were in the bathroom; she sat on the side of the bathtub, giving me some guidance about menstruation. It must have been close to when she left because my heart felt broken wide open, stinging with the acute, unbearable pain of her imminent departure. My younger self found the situation too overwhelming to process, and with no idea how to handle what was taking place, I buried my feelings inside me. I shut myself off from others and built an impenetrable wall around my tender heart.

A mother leaving her children went against the societal norm; it was highly unusual behavior. So much so that my next-door neighbor didn't even believe me when I told her my mum was leaving. In my view of the world, it wasn't how things were supposed to be, and I felt deeply ashamed of her departure. I believed a mother's role was to love her children, look after them, feed them, and support them, no matter what. Quite simply, I couldn't get my head around what was happening; all I could do was put one foot in front of the other and keep breathing. It was a double hit because she left my brother and me with our dad, who I didn't feel safe or happy with.

Another run-in with abandonment occurred when I was sixteen, and John left for college. His departure knocked me flying. I was distraught, and I cried rivers of tears for what seemed like weeks on end. I grieved the loss of him. Even though my rational brain knew that it was time for him to spread his wings and get the heck out of our hometown of Winchester, the wounded parts of me felt as though I'd been abandoned again.

With John gone, I felt alone and very vulnerable to my dad's unpredictable moods. I decided that I needed to be more careful around my dad from then on. Since our mum had left a few years prior, my brother had become a buffer between me and my dad's temper. I was a rather wild teenager and prone to winding my dad up just to piss him off. John stepped in on many occasions to prevent things from getting out of hand between Dad and me, and I felt much safer with John around. We were a team, us against our crappy situation, and we did our best to find the humor in what was happening. With my brother absent, I knew it would be wise, from a self-preservation stance, to pull my head in and stop provoking my dad.

I love my brother fiercely and have always felt an incredibly strong bond with him, even though we're complete opposites in many ways. He is the only other person in the whole wide world who knows exactly how difficult and dysfunctional our life was.

As I mentioned earlier, when we've experienced abandonment, we usually become fearful of being abandoned again and do our utmost to prevent it. People-pleasing tendencies, manipulation, seduction, giving away our power, and making others the authority are just a few ways we attempt to avoid further abandonment. Believing — often unconsciously — that *If they love me, then they won't leave me*, we go out of our way to try and make others love us and never want to leave us. And that's a recipe for disaster and misery for everyone concerned.

Fear played a dominant role in my life as a youngster. Living with my dad created a lot of fear, anxiety, and a general sense of unease. As a teenager, I remember being woken up by him, even on school nights, when he returned from the pub after closing to find the back-door key missing. He'd be so angry, shouting at my brother and me, as he roused us to search for the key. We'd be bleary-eyed from sleep, and my nerves would be on edge as we hunted high and low. We weren't allowed to go back to bed until it was found. He was extremely uptight and unreasonable about lots of things, and it was very stressful and hard to relax when he was around. Even spilling water on the carpet would set him off. Spillages always created a lot of drama with him.

With a mum who'd left home and had virtually no contribution to my life and a dad who was distant, neglectful, and unloving, I grew up with deeply ingrained fears of intimacy and loneliness. Even those who were supposed to love me and look after me weren't to be trusted, and it was safer to distance myself from people to avoid further pain and disappointment.

Even though I was terrified of intimacy and letting people get too close to me, as a teenager, I craved attention, love, and affection from guys. I desperately tried to prove to myself and the world that I mattered and was worthy and lovable. I yearned to be loved, to be looked after, and treasured. But underneath those powerful desires, I was scared that if I got what I wanted, they might abandon me or hurt me. It wasn't a recipe for great relationships.

These fears and longings are very tender, and it's challenging for me to share them with you. However, I believe it's important to air them because I know I'm not alone in having these patterns. Keeping them locked away, avoiding them so we don't have to deal with them, or so no one else sees them, causes significant problems for us rather than improving the situation.

I used to feel ashamed of myself for the ways in which I related to others. It can be very uncomfortable to look honestly at our deepest, most painful fears and their impact on our lives. However, having the courage to explore them helps us peel away layers of dense emotions and loosen unwanted behaviors. It has the power to change our lives for the better.

At one time or another, many of us have pursued emotionally unavailable people in our lives: friends, family members, and lovers. I certainly have; at times, I've turned it into an art form! It's a miserable pattern to find yourself in, leading to intense frustration, disappointment, sadness, anger, and resentment, as well as regarding ourselves as unlovable or unworthy of being loved. At its extreme, when we get locked into a repeating cycle, it can even generate self-loathing and unbearable despair.

I wonder if you can relate to similar patterns of desperately seeking love, approval, and attention from others. Underlying this compulsion, fears of abandonment, intimacy, and loneliness often exist.

You may be free of these fears or well aware of their presence in your life. It's also possible that reading this chapter is beginning to bring them into your conscious awareness. It took me a few decades to become fully aware of the magnitude of my perceived unlovability and unworthiness, and the misery and frustration they created.

My dad passed away suddenly in November 2022. On hearing about his death, I was catapulted into emotional turmoil as grief ripped through every cell of my being.

Consumed by debilitating anguish and in a state of shock, something startling happened to me. It felt as though I'd been given a superpower — a heightened clarity and awareness about various situations in my life. Quite simply, in the blink of an eye, I began to see things differently.

Intense grief can act as a powerful wake-up call, turning our lives upside down and shaking us to our core. Amid the despair, grief can present us with an unexpected gift: a catalyst for much-needed change.

In the weeks that followed, I was gifted with blindingly clear insight into the dissonant energies in a few of my important friendships. I'd known for a long while that something was off, but I had repeatedly brushed the unease aside. My needs weren't being met, and it didn't feel good to me. I'd wanted to make changes but found it incredibly difficult to break free from the familiar, sticky pattern that kept me showing up in the same way, where I regularly felt as if I didn't matter.

With my enhanced clarity, it was plain to see that I needed to enforce stronger boundaries and take better care of myself. It became impossible to continue ignoring these unhealthy dynamics, and I was forced to be brutally honest with myself as I reviewed these friendships.

I realized I had placed some of these friends on a pedestal — making them authority figures in my life and handing over my power to them. I believed they knew more than I did and were wiser than me. This was my old pattern of unworthiness resurfacing, that familiar habit of comparing myself to others and coming up short. In truth, we were equal; no one was "better" or "more spiritually advanced" than the other.

I also admitted to myself how these friends rarely made themselves available to me. The friendships tended to be on their terms, and my efforts to organize phone calls or get-togethers were often ignored. They didn't make time for our friendship and frequently kept themselves just out of reach. When we did connect, they'd give just enough to keep me coming back, always wanting more. I felt powerless to speak up and make the necessary changes. Over the years, I'd made countless excuses for their behavior, and I naively believed the reasons they gave for their unavailability. I kept believing it was a temporary blip that would soon improve. I continued telling myself that we were the closest of friends, and I shared with others how important these relationships were to me.

In the murky depths of my grief, it had become acutely

obvious to me that energetic imbalances existed in these friendships, and I could no longer overlook them. The situation had become intolerable, and I felt compelled to rectify it as soon as possible.

A few months later, I began working with Kate Winch, a transformational coach specializing in Emotional Freedom Technique (EFT), a method that releases emotional stress and energy blockages through tapping on acupressure points. During our first session, she shared something that stopped me in my tracks. She explained the concepts of love addiction, chasing after attention and love from others, and love avoidance, keeping people at a distance and avoiding emotional closeness. These behavior patterns are not limited to intimate relationships. They also show up in other types of relationships: those with family, friends, and work colleagues.

I'd never heard of these ideas before, but as she spoke, I felt an uncomfortable resonance inside every cell in my body. The patterns felt horribly familiar to me. When she suggested that I read *Facing Love Addiction* by Pia Mellody, I knew I needed to buy a copy. When the book arrived in the mail, I read the whole thing cover to cover in a couple of days. I couldn't put it down; I was riveted. This is a valuable book that I highly recommend to you if you sense similar dynamics at work in your life.

Something deep inside of me knew on a visceral level that these patterns of love addiction and avoidance had played a part in what I'd been experiencing in some of my relationships, past and present.

In my eyes, it's unhelpful to call ourselves either a love addict or a love avoidant. In all honesty, I advise against giving ourselves, or others for that matter, any labels at all because it can encourage blame, curtail our ability to take responsibility for our actions, and restrict our model of the world. In truth, virtually everybody runs both of these patterns to some degree. In some situations, we display love-avoidant tendencies; in others, love-addiction behaviors flare up.

There isn't a single behavioral model in the whole universe that adequately describes or explains the complexity of human behavior patterns. However, behavioral models can help us gain greater insight into our own lives, encourage forgiveness and compassion to flow, and assist us in making some profound shifts.

Love addiction and avoidance tendencies often originate in our childhoods from witnessing how our parents related to each other and to us. Their behavior can significantly impact how we relate to others as we grow up. Our early relationships with siblings can also play a significant role in our future relationships. As we reflect on our upbringing, we may see that family members unconsciously played out love-avoidant or love-addictive roles, or both.

Here's an example of circumstances that can contribute to love-avoidant tendencies. If a child was placed on a pedestal by their parent and doted upon, as if they could do no wrong, with the parent handing them the power, the youngster might develop love-avoidant tendencies. They may grow into adulthood behaving as if only their needs matter, doing as they please regardless of any harmful impacts on others, even their spouses and young children. They may shun closeness, be reluctant to look after others, avoid their responsibilities, and sometimes seek love and approval outside their key relationships.

Love-addiction behaviors can be generated in childhood if our emotional needs are not met by our parents. These behaviors can become particularly troublesome if one or both parents were absent in some way — either physically absent because of divorce, death, conscription in wartime, or traveling for their work, or working exceptionally long hours and never being home. Or maybe they were mentally and emotionally absent — physically present but unable to meet the emotional needs of their family, dissociating rather than communicating in loving, supportive, and compassionate ways.

When our caregivers make themselves unavailable in some way, it can intensify love-addiction urges. We may find ourselves craving love and attention from others, sometimes in obsessive ways, and we can easily get caught up in a stubborn pattern-repeating cycle.

There were plenty of awful things that happened in our family life that I'm choosing not to divulge. It wouldn't be appropriate for me to delve into the details of our private lives. So, I'm only sharing things that contribute towards understanding the impact our parents can have on our psyches.

With these patterns of love addiction and love avoidance at play, the scene was set for a miserable and deeply unhealthy family life.

My dad didn't like close, loving relationships; he dodged them at every turn. Being so focused on himself, he preferred to keep a distance from his family. He was emotionally and physically unavailable to us most of the time. He didn't want to be needed or relied upon, and he avoided the role of a loving caretaker like the plague. I remember getting horribly sick with acute tonsilitis regularly as a teenager, and he didn't want to come anywhere near me. I was left to recover on my own because he didn't want to get sick himself. I felt like an inconvenience and an annoyance to him.

My mum wanted more love and attention than she received from my dad. She was so unhappy in her marriage that she left her children and moved in with her boyfriend over 200 miles away.

In their different ways, both of my parents were unavailable to me. Their attention was focused on their marital problems and trying to get their respective needs met. They were so wrapped up in their own universes that I felt like a lost soul, surplus to requirements. I didn't get my emotional needs met, and I was left yearning for love and support.

Shortly after Mum moved out, Dad's girlfriend moved in. I didn't get along with her, and we had plenty of run-ins with each other. I don't recall how long she lived with us, maybe around a year, but it got so bad that I told my dad, "Either she goes, or I do." A few months later, during the car journey home after spending Christmas with Mum in Yorkshire, Dad informed me, "Your archenemy has left." Although my life improved slightly after her departure, it didn't elevate my dad's parenting skills or behavior.

Maybe you can relate to some of what I've discussed. Being aware of the dynamics at play in our familial relationships enables us to notice what is ready to be resolved within our psyches.

From around eleven years of age, my own patterns of love addiction began to fire up, and an intensely strong desire to seek love, approval, and attention from others emerged. Being tall and looking a few years older than my age, I often attracted the attention of older guys. I may have come across to others as tough, rebellious, and a wild spirit, but on the inside, I was naive and lost, wanting to be loved and taken care of, and terrified of being abandoned.

My word, I made some dubious decisions back then, and some of them were downright dangerous. But my compassionate, tender, and wise adult self understands why I behaved the way that I did. I was a lost soul with a lot of emotional baggage. And I had no clue how to love or respect myself.

My most painful, past romantic relationships had been created from these patterns. My fear of abandonment explained why, with only one exception, I'd always been the one to end relationships. Fundamentally, I needed to be the one in control, and I avoided being abandoned by being the one to leave first. And if someone wanted to get too close to me, it would trigger deep discomfort in me, and I'd disconnect from them. These were my strategies for attempting to stay safe and not get hurt.

With a select few of my friends and boyfriends, I relentlessly and enthusiastically chased after what I thought I wanted — incredible closeness — but my recent insight led me to realize that all along, I'd actually been fearful of letting them get too close to me. In a way, I'd been pursuing what I hoped I'd never catch! I played it safe by choosing unavailable people who were least likely to put me to the test in the intimacy stakes, as they weren't capable of that level of connection. So, I played the game of seeking their attention, charming them, seducing them, and claiming that all I wanted was this incredible closeness, when all along I was, in fact, scared to death of it. Had they been willing to experience that level of connection with me, I'm certain I'd have run a mile away, and they would have instantly become unattractive to me as friends or partners.

What I've described falls within the gamut of love-addiction behavior — desperately trying to be loved and accepted in a determined attempt to avoid the agony of being abandoned, and convincing ourselves and others that we desire intimacy and deep connection when, deep down, we're unaware that we're actually scared to death of intimacy. In our eyes, being close to people leaves us open to being heartbroken, and that's to be avoided at all costs. It's a no-win situation that rarely brings much joy or fulfillment.

In contrast, people behaving in love-avoidant ways have a conscious fear of intimacy and an unconscious fear of abandonment. They don't want people to get close to them, so they often distance themselves from others, keeping them at arm's length; meanwhile, underneath it all, outside of their conscious awareness, they're scared of being left — another painful, limited way to live.

This dynamic came into play with my dad when I moved to America. Even though we weren't close, he felt abandoned by me when I left the UK. He pretty much wrote me off and shut me out after that. I'd done the one thing he was most scared of on an unconscious level — I deserted him. I often felt he punished me for it in the years that followed.

I've shared so openly with you about this delicate subject because I've come to see how these commonplace fears of abandonment, intimacy, and loneliness wreak havoc on our relationships with ourselves and others. Exploring these patterns and fears within ourselves can be extremely valuable, enabling powerful shifts to occur.

Can you recognize yourself and your relationships in any shape or form in this chapter? With gentleness, consider if you've pushed people away because you felt uncomfortable by the closeness and felt scared of being hurt. Be honest and kind with yourself and ask if you've sought love, attention, affection, validation, or respect from others in unhealthy ways. And, whatever arises in response to this inquiry, breathe through it all, close your eyes, take a moment, and offer love, support, and compassion to yourself. Take your time with this. Be still a while and breathe deeply, slowly, and fully.

Many of us experience these deep-seated fears and patterns to some degree, so if they feel familiar, please go easy on yourself. Be kind and gentle towards yourself;

remember, it's far from unusual. Most of my clients and many of my friends have struggled with similar issues, and there is nothing to be ashamed of.

There is light at the end of the tunnel, and becoming aware of these fears and patterns is an important first step towards transformation, so be sure to celebrate that.

When we're in these unhealthy patterns, sometimes it can seem impossible to break free from them. Even when we know it isn't good for us, we can feel totally helpless against the intense allure of seeking or avoiding closeness. In a couple of my earlier romantic relationships, I felt devastated when my needs weren't met; my emotions were all over the place, and I didn't feel safe. My inner child was panicking that she would be abandoned, and she tried every possible way to persuade them to love her more, respect her, pay her attention, and so on. It was exhausting, miserable, and futile.

A powerful addictive pattern was at play that I couldn't extract myself from, even though I knew it was so detrimental to my well-being.

I used to be extremely hard on myself about how I let myself be mistreated by others. I believed that the pitiful breadcrumbs of attention were enough to sustain me, that they were better than nothing. So, I put up with it, believing I wasn't worthy of a beautiful, loving relationship. When I realized that my relationship difficulties were partly linked to the influence that my parents' behavior had on me, I was finally able to soften towards myself. It helped me to understand why relationships hadn't always gone so well for me.

Are you familiar with the concept of someone else being a mirror of what's happening inside us? Well, it seems rather amusing to me now, but that had been flashing at me in bright lights, and I'd ignored the signs for years. I sensed a persistent avoidance of intimacy and abandonment in others; yet I hadn't for a moment realized they were just reflecting my own fears back to me. I honestly thought it was their issue, not mine. I believed they were the ones preventing me from experiencing love, affection, and attention, and stopping me from getting what I wanted. It was rather humbling when I realized it was a clear case of projecting onto others what was happening inside of me, but outside of my conscious awareness.

With these complex fears and patterns being hard at work and creating havoc in my life, it's no wonder my journey to self-love was so challenging!

Most of us want to avoid feeling these fears of abandonment, intimacy, and loneliness. We go to great lengths to hide them away or distract ourselves, so we don't experience them.

The key to unlocking a greater capacity for loving ourselves and experiencing a more peaceful existence comes from meeting and welcoming these fears of abandonment, intimacy, and loneliness. It helps to be curious as we do this, maintaining a sense of gentleness together with a willingness to explore what is present.

When these fears arise, rather than pushing them away or distracting yourself, acknowledge them and take some deep breaths. Every thought, emotion, or belief has its own energy field. Take your awareness into the core of that energy field, and be prepared that sensations in the body may occur, some of them very intense. Some common experiences people notice include the following: a raised heart rate, fast, shallow breathing, chest tightness, headache, jaw pain, stomach discomfort, a lump or restriction in the throat, or back pain. Basically, anything can show up! Should you experience any form of physical discomfort, let me reassure you that it's all okay. It's simply the mind trying to tell you that it's not safe to face your fears. Firmly but lovingly, thank it for trying to look after you and let it know that you've got this now and are willing to meet what has arisen.

Thoughts may come thick and fast: stories about the pain, fears, or things that have happened — maybe even descriptions of how uncomfortable you feel or wondering what the heck is going on. There is no need to make the mind the enemy, so without trying to squash your thoughts, simply take your attention off them. They are welcome to come and go as they wish. Refuse to attach to any thoughts or narrative, and keep your focus on the energy field instead. Continue to breathe deeply, slowly, and fully.

Be still. Let the energies move as they wish, whether they are intense or subtle. Exhale anything that is ready to leave your being. You will know when the wave of emotion has subsided. A sense of peacefulness may descend.

These fears and patterns may continue to reappear in our lives from time to time. It's easy to be frustrated or disappointed when they show up again, wishing they'd just disappear. If we try to get rid of them, not only do they continue to hang around, but they also tend to get stronger. Should they return, I suggest opening to the emotional reaction of their resurgence and breathing deeply.

Weakening the influence of our fears takes its own sweet time. Patience is often required. Thankfully, we don't need to eradicate fears entirely for us to feel better. Every single time those fears and patterns are met in loving, curious ways, we release more of our emotional baggage. Our vibration is raised, and we feel better about ourselves, and our lives tend to improve by leaps and bounds.

As healing progresses, we experience greater self-love, compassion, and forgiveness. We release ourselves from the grip of our old patterns of relating to others.

Sometimes, the benefits of our healing process can overflow into our family dynamics, without us even needing to have a conversation with family members. And our relationships can improve on their own, almost as if by osmosis.

We might gain new perspectives and greater clarity, realizing that despite everything, our relatives did the best they could under the circumstances. We may also come to appreciate that their behavior towards us or other family members was shaped by their own conditioning.

If it resonates in our mind's eye, we can direct *Love*, compassion, or healing energies to our entire family — to those who are alive and those who have died, whether the relationships are strained or wonderful. Potent healing can result from this beautiful offering.

On a warm autumnal afternoon, while walking my dog at Sherwood Island State Park, my guides shared some valuable insights with me.

As I strode along the gravel path, with the ocean sparkling in front of me, my guides revealed that I'd chased after something that no one was able to give me. It had consistently remained just out of reach. My quest for genuine, profound connections was unachievable, and it would only continue to create frustration, sadness, anger, and disappointment for me.

I'd yearned for it with friends, family, and romantic relationships. At times, it had been a compelling, intense, unmet longing.

My guides shared that my intimacy issues with others hadn't been at the heart of the matter. I was, in fact, scared of being intimate with myself, of truly loving myself just as I was, with all my perceived imperfections. Hearing that, I stood still for a moment, letting their revelations sink in. I sensed the undeniable truth that lay in their words.

As I continued walking, an even deeper realization appeared. My guides showed me that, in addition to being fearful of being intimate with myself, I was also scared of being truly intimate with the Divine. I knew they'd hit the nail on the head with this one too. My cells were vibrating with the accuracy of their message.

Sure, I connected with the Divine regularly, but mainly when trouble appeared in my life, and I needed help navigating problems. I'd tap in for insights and guidance, then jump right back out into regular life and remain disconnected from the Divine for most of my day.

Basically, I only reached out when I needed something. I wasn't devoting time to nurturing my love affair with the Divine. It was meant to be a two-way relationship, and I wasn't bringing much to the party.

I'd believed myself wholeheartedly when I'd said in the past that I'd surrendered to *Love*. But the truth was, I could feel the disparity between the amount I'd actually surrendered — likened to a very short, half-hearted jog — and total surrender, best illustrated by taking a long, hard run up and jumping off a cliff.

That day, I discovered that at the core of this fear of intimacy with others lay an inability to love myself, warts and all, and a reluctance to surrender fully to the Divine. My guides showed me that all the *Love* and intimacy I'd ever desired was right here, inside of me, so close that I'd been overlooking it. Thankfully, they told me, I never again needed to search outside of myself to find it. The exhausting, futile chase was over.

I was shown that *Love* is always available to me in my connection to my inner self and the Divine. All that is required is to turn inward, bring my awareness gently into my heart, and be still. I laughed out loud and glowed radiantly as I bathed in the potent energies that flowed through every particle of my being. Thank you Divine; what a gift!

The same treasure awaits you, too.

# 3

# WE'RE NOT WHO WE THINK WE ARE

Our beliefs have a gigantic effect on the degree to which we're able to open into self-love. If we believe ourselves to be unlovable or unworthy of being loved, it will limit our ability to love ourselves or form loving, healthy relationships. Our beliefs create our reality, meaning that what we believe to be true tends to show up in our external lives with bells and whistles. If we believe things always go wrong, then guess what? They usually do.

Beliefs are generated by our life experiences and conditioning from our parents, teachers, and other authority figures in our lives. It's well documented that under the age of about seven, we accept, without question, the thoughts, beliefs, and behaviors of those around us. We're like little sponges, soaking up everything we're witnessing. In fact, this absorption occurs even before our birth, as we float inside our mother's womb.

We take on the beliefs and behaviors of others as our own, and they exert an enormous influence over how we perceive ourselves and our relationships, and how our lives unfold.

We craft beliefs about ourselves like *I'm worthless; I'm unlovable; It's not okay to be angry; I need to please others to stay safe; I don't matter; No one cares about me; Life is tough; Nothing ever goes right for me;* and so on.

Core beliefs of unworthiness and unlovability had enormous negative impacts on my life. They limited my ability to let my full potential blossom and feel joyful, and they made relationships extremely challenging for me.

Limiting beliefs can trip us up big time in a multitude of ways, diminishing our light and curtailing our enjoyment of life.

When we hold a painful belief about ourselves, like *I'm not smart enough*, we view our lives through the lens of that belief. We scan our experiences for evidence of not being smart enough. Humans are experts at unconsciously seeking proof to further reinforce our beliefs. When we sense our belief is validated, we say to ourselves, *See, I told you I wasn't smart enough!* Every time we do this, the original belief becomes more deeply ingrained in our psyche, and we become more convinced that it is true.

That might sound a bit bonkers to some of you. Nevertheless, it happens. It's often part of a survival strategy, a misplaced attempt to prevent us from taking risks and trying to keep us away from harm.

What are some of your persistent limiting beliefs about yourself? In contrast, can you think of some supportive beliefs you hold about life or yourself? What is your unique blend of beliefs?

We all have a mixed bag of beliefs. Positive ones make us feel good and create wonderful things in our lives, while painful beliefs tend to hold us back and generate some form of suffering.

Some of our beliefs are deeply familiar to us, and we know them well, regardless of whether we like them or not. Others are hidden from our conscious awareness.

When tricky things happen in our lives, it can be a great time to identify associated unconscious beliefs. By looking honestly at what is happening, we often discover a common thought stream running through our experiences. By pausing and being curious, we can begin to uncover the troublesome beliefs underlying our behavior.

If nothing bubbles up, sometimes it's helpful to ask: *What would I need to believe about myself (or the world) in order to think or behave that way?* and then wait to see what arises. It's best to stay out of our analytical mind and open our awareness in every direction, letting the answers come to us, rather than desperately trying to hunt them down.

Notice the impact that beliefs have on your inner world. Bring one of yours to mind, and notice the effect it has on your body as you think about it. Some might make you tense and tighten or create a sense of dread in your stomach. Others will feel great, with a spacious, delicious flavor. The effects on our body go way beyond what we can discern regarding physical sensations. Biochemical changes abound. When we consistently believe our negative beliefs over protracted periods of time, it can contribute to significant health issues.

Here's a story about the power of beliefs and our ability to change them.

By my mid-thirties, I'd spent nine years at home, bringing up my children, and I made a brave decision. I'd been doing my very best to be a perfect wife, mother, homemaker, and gardener. I'd lost a lot of confidence through those years. More than that, I'd lost the sense of who I was because I'd worn so many masks playing the roles of who I thought I should be. Deep-seated beliefs abounded about my profound unworthiness and inability to get back into the working world in a meaningful way, coupled with beliefs that I didn't matter and my needs weren't important. I kind of knew those beliefs were there. Now and then, they'd pop their heads up above the wall, and I'd bat them away again without addressing them.

My courageous decision? I signed up for a year-long, intensive training program in London to become a certified Pilates instructor. That decision seems so small now, compared to the things I've done since then, but at the time, it took me several months to muster up the confidence to go for it.

There I was, on the first day of the course, in Neal's Yard in Covent Garden, a characterful and beautiful part of London with colorful, painted doors, tall brick buildings, and window boxes overflowing with scented flowers. The class was held in an airy training room with wide pine floorboards, white walls, and various Pilates paraphernalia stored neatly in shelving units against the walls. We sat in a circle on the floor, the upright fans buzzing as they whizzed around to keep us cool. Welcome to hot days in England without air-conditioning! One by one we introduced ourselves and were asked to say something about our lives.

I blushed more and more intensely the closer it got to being my turn to speak — that familiar and most unwelcome sensation of heat building up to the levels of a pizza oven awaiting the arrival of a tasty pepperoni pizza. It felt like I was back in school again as a youngster. Blushing had plagued me then, and I was teased by teachers, friends, and other students for years. Here in this moment, I suspected that I was already most likely the color of a strawberry. That always made the panic worse, feeling the heat and imagining the color of my face. I was dreading the moment I would have to share. When I did, the only thing that came out of my mouth was, "Hi, I'm Rachel, and I'm a stay-at-home mum."

Even though I had a couple of degrees, and I'd worked as a hydrologist and a business-development executive, the years of staying at home had dented my confidence. I didn't feel worthy of being there, doubted my ability to do well in the course, and was extremely daunted by the task ahead of me.

That moment was a cataclysmic wake-up call. I was horrified and full of despair as I uttered those words and heard myself. *What had become of me? Who was this person with no self-confidence? Is that all I can say about myself?*

It was devastating, and I was hard on myself about it. The inner critic was throwing a party. But as it turned out, it was a tremendous gift. I got to see those beliefs that I'd been brushing off. They were right there, in my face, clear as day. Becoming aware of my restrictive beliefs and feeling so despondent and unworthy created a decisive turning point in my life.

I went on to thrive in the course. I thoroughly enjoyed teaching clients. Before the training, I didn't like getting physically close to people and avoided touching them, but as a trainee Pilates instructor, I had no choice — I had to do it. Using my hands to guide clients and adjust their positions to build awareness was essential. The whole experience, from start to finish, set me on an exciting new trajectory in my life. The rebirth began.

I learned about and experienced the mind-body connection, being completely present in the moment, gaining body awareness, and being able to focus on activating or relaxing even teeny-tiny muscles in the body. Who knew that this level of focus could make you feel calmer and more peaceful, allowing you to leave your daily troubles and worries far behind and departing class with a smile on your face and a skip in your step?

I gave that training course my all; ultimately, it was such an empowering experience that it reignited my self-confidence. Those pesky beliefs began shifting into more resourceful, supportive ones. I'd proved to myself that I could do it and was incredibly proud of myself.

I've come to realize that it's very common for women

to lose their sense of who they really are when they play the roles of wife and mother, and their confidence levels, self-belief, and self-worth are often at rock bottom. They can find themselves having a full-blown identity crisis and struggling to find their way back to feeling good about themselves, loving themselves, and putting themselves first. It's ridiculously tough to break out of the pattern and the expectation that women should look after everyone else first: their husbands, their children, the pets, the home, and their work life, before making quality time for themselves.

This story about my Pilates training has inspired many female friends and clients to embark on new paths and careers, step outside their comfort zone, and find a way to prioritize themselves and swim in the deep waters of self-love.

Two traumatic accidents happened when I was younger than three. The end of my finger was cut off in a sliding door, and my face was severely burned when boiling custard spilled onto me from a saucepan on the stovetop. I don't have clear memories of either of those events. But I've seen a photo of me toddling around, looking like an Egyptian mummy with bandages over a large portion of my face. Even though I didn't have access to those specific memories, my body held onto the energetic pattern of terror, pain, and shock.

My mum was present when both of those accidents happened. She'd accidentally closed the sliding door on my finger. And she'd been supervising me as I stood on a stool stirring the boiling custard.

From those experiences, I created specific beliefs: *The world isn't a safe place; I need to be on guard; and I can't trust anyone to look after me.* In that perpetual state of high alert, my stress response remained switched ON most of the time.

Over the years, I've struggled with beliefs about some of my physical characteristics that resulted from accidents or surgery. At times, I regarded myself as maimed and flawed and felt rather self-conscious about these features. Sometimes, they really bugged me, usually when I was feeling down about myself or when I fell into the trap of comparing myself to perceived perfection in others and believing myself to be inferior.

So, from that sliding door accident, the end of one of my fingers is missing, the ring finger on my right hand. It's noticeably shorter and has a unique curved shape to it. I have a scar on my inner arm that marks the spot where a skin graft was taken to place some skin on the end of my damaged finger. Then there's my big toenail on my left foot. It looks rather weird as I had the toenail surgically removed twice when I was about eleven years old.

That toenail reminds me of how bad my dad was at looking after me. I struggled for ages with my foot; it was excruciatingly painful, and it got into a right old state. Even though he was writing notes to excuse me from sports at school, he did little to step in and get me the care I needed. After the second surgery, the nail grew back in a distinctive manner, with a personality all of its own. Moving on, I have a capped front tooth because a horse head-butted me, and I have a scar on my face from surgery to remove skin cancer.

I've experienced my fair share of accidents and sports injuries. I've cracked my head open on a massive wooden beam in a barn, cut open the inside of my wrist on a glass panel of a door, suffered from extensive burns to my face in the boiling custard incident, ripped my knee open in a motorbike accident, repeatedly damaged my right ankle, torn my plantaris muscle in my leg playing tennis, and have fallen off a multitude of horses and bikes in my time. While writing this book, I was busy adding a couple of broken toes to my list of accidents.

I realized those unhealthy beliefs I'd held about how I looked weren't true. I'm beautiful and perfect in my imperfections. Healing these beliefs and accepting my finger, toe, face, and tooth have been important in my journey to wholeness. They give me stories to tell and add to my individuality and character. Quite simply, they represent parts of my history and add color to my life.

We feel so much better about ourselves when we stop wishing that our bodies looked a certain way or performed as we believe they should, or wishing that those accidents or surgeries had never happened, and instead, accept them just as they are. From this place of acceptance, we can feel loving compassion towards ourselves for everything our bodies have experienced.

There is a powerful mindset that runs through my birth family: Everything always goes wrong, and even the most minor problems are treated as complete nightmares.

Here's a perfect example of the pattern at play. I was dragged into one of my mum's crazy and intense over-reactions when I was a young teenager. My dad had gone away for a few days, and she'd come to visit. During a shopping expedition to Southampton, she bought me a pair of colorful wooden earrings. They were inexpensive and nothing fancy, but they caught my eye. I then proceeded to lose them while we were out on the shopping trip. They didn't even make it home with me. I was sad about losing them but decided to focus on accepting my minor loss. Instead of making me feel better and putting it into perspective, my mum went completely berserk, shouting at me, reprimanding me, and telling me over and over how awful the situation was, how careless I was, and how I didn't look after things or value them. I felt crushed and as though I was a wasteful, terrible, and irresponsible person.

Following family tradition, I began responding in this unhealthy way to the blips in my life. Doing so caused me considerable problems, and sadly, it often involved others being caught up in my whirlwind of self-abuse.

During a summer spent in Chicago, I accidentally dropped my wallet while getting out of a taxi. It contained my bank and credit cards and about two hundred dollars in cash. You'd have thought the world had ended;

the self-abuse that followed was so distressing — not just for me but also for my husband, kids, and mother-in-law, Diana, who was visiting from England. They all witnessed my screaming, wailing, and shouting. It was ugly. I had no idea how crazy my response to small problems was until Diana witnessed this event. She gently and lovingly tried to talk to me rationally about how it was just an accident, and everything would be okay.

It took me many painful months of beating myself up before I finally stopped blaming myself for this incident. Judgmental beliefs like *I should have been more careful!; I'm such an idiot!; I'm so stupid!; I'm so careless!;* and *This is a complete disaster!* kept going round and round in my head. I tortured myself and put my stress levels through the roof.

It even happened with food. A thoughtful and generous friend gave me some delicious raisin cinnamon bagels, my favorite flavor, from the best bagel store near where we'd lived in New Jersey. She'd sent them with her son Robbie, who'd flown down to Charlotte, North Carolina, to visit us, and I was thrilled to receive them. Yes, it's true — I get very excited about food — I'm a massive foodie.

When the bagels arrived with Robbie, I put them into the overflow freezer in my garage to make them last for a while. By a stroke of bad luck, a week or so later, the electrical circuit in the garage tripped, turning the freezer off. By the time I noticed that the freezer wasn't working, its entire contents had defrosted. My beloved bagels were ruined and inedible. I completely overreacted to that; my response was so extreme you'd have thought someone had died. In the middle of my fury, I gained access to a bird's eye view of how ridiculous my behavior was, but I still couldn't stop myself.

It took me many years to shake off this way of responding to life's tricky moments. Most of the time, I'm able to react in a level-headed manner, albeit with some exasperated sighing and frequently muttering profanities. Once in a blue moon, I still get highly agitated, but I usually bounce back to sanity quickly and find that I'm able to recenter myself with relative ease.

These disproportionate responses emanated from limiting beliefs I'd picked up from my childhood years, which were working away behind the scenes to cause mayhem and misery. The beliefs were just thoughts with no basis in reality. The only time they caused trouble for me was when I believed them to be true and gave my power away to them. The good news is that we are not victims of our beliefs; they are not fixed or written in stone, and we can clear them to create more of what we want in our lives.

Although it can be subtle, we often take on our tightly held beliefs as part of our identity. Along the lines of *I'm unlovable. That's who I am . . . unlovable.* Despite what we may think, beliefs are not personal. They are just energy, tied up in a familiar thought form. Even those strongly ingrained beliefs are not you; they do not define you and may be untrue.

Our limiting beliefs are not the enemy — far from it. They are a potent driving force that fuels behaviors aimed at keeping us safe and controlling our lives to prevent us from getting hurt. Beliefs are part of our powerful survival strategies. But instead of helping us, limiting beliefs can cause us a lot of pain and limitation, keeping us stuck or going around in exhausting circles.

Over the years, I've learned various tools and techniques to assist my clients and myself in clearing unproductive beliefs. Some of them are complex processes with numerous steps and requiring assistance from a practitioner. Others are straightforward, quick, and easy to use on the go. These days, I'm a fan of simplicity and approaches we can use on our own to make a big difference. Then, as life happens and problematic beliefs appear, we can deal with them there and then, removing obstacles and clearing the way forward so we can thrive.

It can be helpful to make a list of your painful beliefs as you become aware of them. Beliefs can be sneaky. They are rarely present all the time; they flit in and out of our awareness. Even when they have disappeared back into the depths of our unconscious mind, they continue to exert a powerful influence. Keeping an ongoing list of them can help us to stay focused as we work through our troublesome beliefs. Each time we review our list, we get a welcome dopamine hit by noticing those that have weakened or become irrelevant. It feels great to mark our progress and celebrate how much better we feel.

Before we dive into some great clearing tools, bear in mind that sometimes our beliefs are weakened or even disappear completely as a result of us rising to the challenge and doing something that flies in the face of our fears. My Pilates story is an excellent example of this. We may prove our old beliefs to be false and create new beliefs like *I'm capable; I'm smart;* and *I can do this.* I will add that sometimes, it can be context-driven. We may believe our success was limited to that event, doubting our abilities if we try to do something else. If the belief continues to stubbornly impact us, using a tool may prove beneficial.

Here are three of my current preferred approaches for loosening or clearing limiting beliefs that I use regularly. If any resonate with you, experiment in a playful way with one of your own painful beliefs to create some welcome, lasting shifts for yourself.

Some of you will be more than happy to roll up your sleeves, elicit your beliefs, and use these tools on your own. And some of you will feel more comfortable working with a therapist or a practitioner of some kind. Tune into your inner guidance and do what feels most suitable and comfortable for you.

### ACCEPTANCE & COMMITMENT THERAPY (ACT) TOOLS

ACT tools were developed by Dr. Stephen C. Hayes, a clinical psychologist, in the 1980s. Some of his approaches may seem deceptively straightforward, but they can be extraordinarily effective in loosening beliefs or rendering them powerless. *ACT Made Simple* (Second Edition), by Russ Harris, does a superb job of explaining ACT and offers plenty of great examples of these techniques in action.

One of my favorites, which falls under the umbrella of cognitive defusion, is brilliant at helping us create distance between ourselves and our thoughts. Harris refers to this technique as "I'm having the thought that...". In a nutshell, you take one of your unpleasant thoughts, such as "Everyone is out to get me," and add "I'm having the thought that..." in front of the limiting belief, and then say it aloud. So, using my example, the full statement would be: "I'm having the thought that everyone is out to get me." Then you take a moment to notice how that feels inside of you.

Next, add, "I'm noticing that I'm having the thought that..." in front of the same belief and say the whole statement. In this case, it would be: "I'm noticing that I'm having the thought that everyone is out to get me."

After completing these steps, take a few moments to bring your awareness inside your body and see if your perspective on that old belief has shifted. Usually, the belief feels further away, less intense, and somehow less significant.

It may seem hard to believe, but it's truly astonishing how much better we can feel when we use this simple approach to create distance from our thoughts. If this technique resonates with you, I highly recommend checking out Harris's book for more insights.

## THE WORK BY BYRON KATIE

In her book, *A Mind at Home with Itself*, spiritual teacher Byron Katie says, "I realized that when I believed my thoughts, I suffered, but that when I didn't believe them, I didn't suffer, and that this is true for every human being.

Freedom is as simple as that."

"The Work" is a powerful approach created by Byron Katie, which involves questioning our beliefs instead of automatically believing them to be true. Using four potent questions, we explore the accuracy of our thoughts. We experience how we think, feel, and behave when we hold a specific belief, and then we consider who we would be without it. A key aspect of the process is developing what she calls "turnarounds" — alternative, more resourceful, or enlightening beliefs that may be just as true, or even truer, than the original thought.

I use this method frequently with my clients, and it's an integral part of my own personal toolbox. It effectively loosens or releases troublesome beliefs by opening us up to new perspectives and possibilities. However, it's important to note that while this method is a gem for many, it isn't everyone's cup of tea. If it doesn't resonate with you, simply try a different technique instead.

Katie's book, *Loving What Is: Four Questions That Can Change Your Life*, is an invaluable resource for learning and understanding The Work. For further information, you can also visit her website, which I've listed in a resources page on my website. You'll find the link to that in the "Golden Nuggets" section at the back of this book.

## EMOTIONAL FREEDOM TECHNIQUE (EFT)

I'm a huge fan of EFT, also known as tapping. Are you familiar with it? I've been an enthusiastic tapper for almost two decades now.

Many years ago, I used my tapping skills with a woman during a flight. She was terrified of flying, and when she sat down next to me, she warned me that she would probably throw up. To avoid that scenario, for both of our sakes, I asked if she was open to tapping to help her relax. Thankfully, she was all for it. I led her through a few rounds of tapping, and she was astounded when her deep-seated fear of flying disappeared in less than half an hour. After landing, my fellow passenger was ecstatic, heaping praise and gratitude on me. She shared how amazing she thought I was with my teenage daughter, who responded with a well-practiced roll of the eyes!

If you're new to tapping, in essence, it's a simple and easy technique that involves gently tapping with your fingertips on specific points of the body, while focusing on releasing unwanted thoughts and emotions, and replacing them with positive alternatives. When you'd like to experience some relief from problematic issues, you begin the tapping process by spending a little time identifying the key issues at play. That means determining what you'd like to let go of, including any limiting beliefs and painful emotions, and what you'd like to experience more of, for example, joy, confidence, and self-love. To assist you in staying focused as you tap, it may help you if you create a list of the different aspects, what you wish to release, and what you'd like to experience, to refer to at a glance as you proceed.

Then you allocate a numerical value out of ten to represent the intensity of your issue, with ten being the most intense. This acts as a barometer, showing you how strong this particular pattern or belief is in your psyche. Next, using the first two fingers of both hands, you tap on a series of specific acupressure points in a particular sequence. As you tap, you state out loud what you want to release. After a while, you'll start to bore yourself with your venting, and that's your cue to begin focusing on what you wish to experience instead.

Often, it takes a few rounds of tapping to create the desired effect. After each round, to discern your progress, you recheck the intensity number associated with your original belief or issue. You'll discover to your delight that the number reduces as these patterns loosen in your energetic being. It's not necessary to get it all the way down to zero — a one, two, or three may bring tremendous relief and a shift in consciousness.

Tapping works fast and can improve every aspect of our lives. I particularly love that it works even if someone is skeptical about its efficacy. I've used tapping for all kinds of things — from improving my tennis game to enhancing my relationships, clearing self-doubt and fear, and boosting my self-confidence and creativity. You'll find some excellent EFT resources on my website. There's a direct link to that valuable resource in the "Golden Nuggets" section of this book.

Tapping is brilliant. If you need privacy in a stressful moment, you can nip to the bathroom and tap yourself into a calm state. Tap in bed, in the bath, in the waiting room at the dentist's office, out walking, or while stuck in traffic — you get the idea!

In this chapter, I've mainly focused on limiting beliefs because they can cause tremendous difficulties in our lives. As we've already heard that our beliefs create our reality, I would be remiss to exclude utilizing the power of positive beliefs. This approach works best when we get ourselves into a deep state of relaxation before repeating affirming thoughts. The best results occur when we connect with the feeling states of what we wish to experience. We need to totally convince ourselves that it's true, playing at 100 percent. Delusional? Maybe! But it works!

A few years ago, I had four wisdom teeth removed. I'd seen the kids go through that surgery. It was a painful recovery, and their faces were bruised and swollen. So, I decided to play around with having a better experience than that. Before the surgery, I kept telling myself that my jaw would feel fine afterward and that my face would be unaffected. It worked a treat! I didn't need even a single Advil after the anesthetic had worn off. When I started to feel a sensation building in my jaw, I just reminded myself with love, kindness, and firmness: *Oh no, remember? My jaw is relaxed and happy, and my recovery is quick and easy.* Then, the sensation immediately subsided. I had no swelling or bruising. It was a fascinating experiment.

If you decide to use this approach, remember it's crucial that you get yourself into a suggestible state of mind and believe it completely!

I use the same technique, which is self-hypnosis, to prevent jet lag. I must share that as a mini-workshop someday!

Clearing painful beliefs and employing supportive and nourishing ones can be an extremely important part of healing from whatever has occurred in our lives. It can help us to open into loving ourselves and deepening our connection to our inner selves.

However, I'm not suggesting we look at everything through rose-tinted glasses. Terrible, traumatic things may have happened. What I'm saying is that we have the power to refuse to believe the stories we tell ourselves about those events and what we might be making them mean about us. Transforming our beliefs supports us on every level of our being and encourages our energy to flow more freely.

With love and compassion, I encourage you to question your beliefs. They are not who we are; they are simply energy, and when we refuse to believe our painful thoughts, the truth sets us free. What a blessed relief!

# 4

# SO MANY WAYS TO CRACK AN EGG

All of us have emotional wounds of some kind, to differing degrees. Many of us have experienced painful trauma that creates all kinds of problems in our lives. And for those of us with "mother wounds," the trauma can be particularly difficult to deal with. Maybe it's because our mothers carried us in their wombs and were the ones we believed would love and care for us no matter what. When they die prematurely, abandon us, neglect us, or abuse us, it can be extraordinarily hard to heal, leaving us feeling unlovable, unworthy, and alone in the world.

I've put a lot of time, energy, and resources into healing from my childhood experiences. Since 2005, with a curious and tenacious spirit, I've seen a multitude of healers and various practitioners in my quest to feel better. I've experienced many modalities, including Reiki, Neuro-Linguistic Programming (NLP), Time Line Therapy™, shamanic practices, hypnosis, meridian tapping, craniosacral therapy, massage, sound healing, breathwork, The Journey™ processes, Non-Personal Awareness® (NPA®), Eye Movement Desensitization and Reprocessing (EMDR), integrative muscle therapy, Rolfing, Akashic Record consultations, acupuncture, healing waters through Healers

Who Share, life coaching, psychic readings, Harmonic Egg™ sessions, and distant healings with John of God.

That isn't a complete list either; there are others I've since forgotten about or totally dismissed! You may be relieved to hear that you don't need to do all, or any, of these to feel better. Please know I'm not trying to convince you of any specific idea or approach.

My intention is to offer you loving support for your own healing path, whatever direction you decide to take.

I usually turn to energy medicine for healing before visiting a medical doctor or pursuing conventional medical treatment because I like to focus on ways to boost my body's innate ability to heal itself. That's just my way, and I'm not for one millisecond suggesting what kind of treatment you should have. Quite simply, at all times, do what feels best for you. Medical doctors, surgery, medications, therapy, or energy-healing modalities — you're the expert on you. So, trust that only you know what the best approach is for you.

When I moved to America, a troublesome health problem appeared, and it escalated over the next few years. The treatment options suggested by a medical doctor didn't feel good to me. Not a bone in my body wanted medication or surgery, so I politely refused them. I was determined to find a way to heal naturally, using energy-healing approaches. I sensed that a strong, energetic component

lay at the core of my ailment, a heady mix of abandonment, unlovability, unworthiness, and powerlessness.
And I believed energy medicine was the best way to bring
my body back into balance and harmony. At this time in
my life, on the spectrum of healing — with energy healing
at one end and mainstream medicine on the other — I sat
steadfastly in the camp of energy medicine. I was closed off
to much of what conventional medicine had to offer.

After a couple of years of no improvement, I was feeling
increasingly stressed and hopeless about my situation, but
I remained determined to find a natural way for my body
to heal itself.

Around this time, I met someone who acted as a surrogate by visiting John of God, a famous medium and
spiritual healer based in Brazil, to seek healing on behalf
of others. After seeing a person's photo and hearing about
their healing intentions, John of God would direct healing energies to them from the entities he channeled. I was
curious about the process and hopeful that a distant healing might help me, so I signed up.

As instructed, I wore white on the day of the healing
and rested in bed, remaining there until the next day. I was
taken aback by what happened. I felt like I'd been plugged
into the electricity supply. Intense waves of energy surged
through my system, ebbing and flowing as the hours
passed. I continually surrendered, focusing on relaxing
my body and letting the energies flow through me. It was
pretty wild, and I was completely wiped out for a few days
afterward. When she returned from Brazil, my surrogate

gave me some water blessed by John of God for me to drink to continue the healing.

Did it work? Well, my problem completely vanished, or at least it did until the blessed water ran out, and then it came back with a vengeance. Although I was disappointed, something remarkable and unexpected happened that led to the resolution of my problem. To my astonishment, my mindset on conventional treatment had shifted massively, and I suddenly became downright enthusiastic and optimistic about having surgery. That was a complete miracle as far as I was concerned! I'd moved from one end of the healing spectrum, insisting that only energy medicine would do, to a balanced, centered place, where I embraced both approaches to healing — a combination of the latest medical practices and energetic modalities. My choice to have surgery didn't come from a despondent place where I'd given up and thought it was my only option. No, no, no. It wasn't a defeatist energy behind my decision; it was an empowered one, and it felt good.

A couple of nights before my procedure, some radiant, dear soul sisters conducted a powerful, beautiful healing ceremony with immense *Love* and Grace. I received hands-on healing, and they showered me with fragrant rose petals. In absolute alignment with my treatment choice, surgery was straightforward, and I healed quickly with no need for pain relief. My health issue was resolved.

So, I encourage you to stay open to how healing will occur. Sometimes, healing appears as a shift in our consciousness that generates new ways of behaving, enabling new possibilities for physical healing to emerge.

I discovered a few years after my distant healing with John of God that he's currently in prison, serving a long sentence after being found guilty of raping and sexually abusing women at his casa. I was unaware of any issues when I signed up to work with him.

One of the greatest lessons that emerged from my healing path and from working with clients is that there is no specific path through healing that will guarantee relief from suffering. I'm not offering you a step-by-step, foolproof healing process that works for everyone with a traumatic past. In my opinion, to do so would be disingenuous, misleading, and egotistical. The truth is, what's worked for me, or anyone else for that matter, may not benefit you.

Healing happens differently for each of us, so comparing ourselves to others is pointless. We're unique beings, products of our own upbringing, conditioning, experiences, and genetics, each with our own vibrations, who came to this current incarnation with specific areas for soul evolution and growth, specific lessons to learn, and purposes to fulfill. Approaches and practitioners that resonate with some people won't be a good fit for others. In the "Alchemy Tools" section at the back of this book, you'll find my favorite methods for discerning how to make choices in alignment with our highest good. You can use those methods for any situation, including deciding on doctors, healers, and treatment.

A tiny number of people experience instantaneous spiritual awakenings and/or healings and spontaneously exist in a blissed-out state of oneness. Ramana Maharshi, Byron Katie, Anita Moorjani, and Eckert Tolle are good examples. But most of us, including myself, tend to experience incremental shifts over time as we heal or awaken. Little by little, layers of wounds are peeled away as stuck energies inside of us become ripe for resolution, healing, and liberation. Layers containing old patterns, limiting beliefs, and painful emotions, including hurt, anger, sadness, grief, self-hatred, despair, humiliation, regret, disappointment, shame, or guilt, are released from our bodies and energy fields.

Over time, we spiral progressively deeper into our core wounds, allowing the potential for more of our suffering to be liberated. Thankfully, for the vast majority of us, we only tend to unearth and deal with what our nervous system can handle at any given time. This is our body's wisdom at play, looking after us. If we were to take on too much at once, it could overwhelm our system, making it impossible to function in everyday human life.

Oh, and be prepared for issues that you thought you'd "healed" coming back and biting you on the arse. We can be shouting at the Universe: *Not this again! I thought I'd sorted this out!*; or *I'm so sick of this showing up and messing up my life!* It can cause us considerable suffering because it feels outside of our control, and we believe we'll never be free of it. Rather than sitting in victimhood and resisting it, know a resurgence of painful issues is to be expected now and then. With deep kindness towards yourself, meet and celebrate its presence. It's simply a sign of the spiral going deeper and deeper, with new aspects appearing for resolution that were previously inaccessible to us, hidden out of sight, and buried deeply within our psyche.

From my perspective, healing never reaches completion. So, it's in our best interests to let go of the false belief that one day we'll be 100 percent "fixed." The truth is, if we look deep enough, we'll always find more unhealthy patterns or things that we believe still need healing. This search can become a habit or, at its extreme, can morph into an obsession. We can create additional frustration, impatience, suffering, and misery for ourselves when we believe we're irrevocably damaged in some way and focus on what still needs healing.

It's common to fall into the trap of believing that we'll be happy only when we've healed ourselves completely — when we've reached that fantasy future destination that always seems just out of our grasp. In effect, we're telling ourselves that wherever we are right now is unacceptable. We're resisting what is. Are you familiar with Carl Jung's famous quote: "What you resist persists"? Our suffering lingers when we push against our wounds, wishing we were fully healed rather than accepting and embracing what is present for us. So, just as you are, at whatever stage of your healing journey, please let me reassure you that it's all okay. You are whole just as you are. Be gentle and patient with yourself, and do your best to let go of unrealistic expectations about your journey.

The marvelous news is that although we may never reach the unachievable goal of being 100 percent healed, we can still transform our lives and feel massively better about ourselves and our past and present. As healing progresses, the ways in which we respond to life's challenges will likely change. When the going gets tough, we tend to find ourselves being more flexible, accepting, and loving, bouncing back more quickly from stressful situations and returning to a grounded, balanced, and centered state with relative ease.

Overhearing my self-talk and questioning my thoughts have helped me immensely. Our minds create all kinds of thoughts and beliefs. Most of them aren't even necessarily true, just our versions of reality. We create stories continually with our over-active, fearful minds. When we believe them, these narratives cause us varying degrees of suffering, especially when we repeatedly run them through our minds, reminding ourselves over and over again of what hurts or who did what to whom.

When I began tuning into my inner narrative, I discovered it was comprised of falsehoods, judgment, blame, and negativity. Pretty shocking! Becoming aware of my thoughts enabled me to pause the thought stream, take a good look at what I was thinking about, and question it all, creating a powerful pattern interrupt and putting the brakes on automatically believing my thoughts to be true. It created space inside of me, enabling me to see things differently and to view events and people from a broader, more loving, compassionate, and resourceful perspective. From there, new possibilities became available to me, and I tended to feel better about myself and my life. In this spaciousness, a moment of choice revealed itself. In this pause, a space opened up where I had the ability to choose calming, joyful thoughts instead of miserable stories and negative thoughts.

When we obsessively remind ourselves about our suffering or our problematic health conditions, we're keeping them alive energetically, concretizing them in our bodies and energy fields, making it harder for healing to take place. On the other hand, by accepting and embracing how we feel and any dis-ease in our bodies, releasing resistance, and seeing the body as healed and ourselves as peaceful and joyful, we're strengthening our body's natural ability to heal itself.

I know from personal experience how tough it can be to accept what's happened to us, our medical challenges, and the origins of them. Our conscious minds, also known as our egoic minds, strive to be in control, wanting things to be different from how they are and trying to force desired outcomes. The ego will often fight acceptance by saying, *Well, terrible things did happen to me. I can't pretend they didn't. Are you mad? Just give it a hug?!!* Or *I have stomach issues. It hurts, and I'm worried about it, so of course, I keep thinking about it. I have good reason to.* Think of it this way: We're not denying what is; we're changing how we respond, opening up new opportunities for healing and soul evolution.

It's helpful to remember that our egoic minds are in fact trying to keep us safe, attempting to protect us. Speak to your ego self as if it were a small child; reassure this part of you by connecting with it and letting it know that you're on its side, asking if it wants to communicate something to you. Listen intently to anything it shares in response, reassuring it by letting it know you will look after it. It can be helpful to say, *I've got you, so you can relax and rest.* Then, embrace and love your conscious mind along with what has been causing problems or pain. This practice will boost your healing process and deepen your experience of loving yourself.

Many of us would love to know how long it will take to feel noticeably lighter and brighter so that our lives can improve immeasurably. It'll take as long as it takes; it might be quick, take a long while, or fall somewhere between the two. When we let ourselves exist in the state of not knowing, being curious and keeping an open mind while surrendering and going with the flow, it may not speed things up, but it certainly feels better and improves the quality of our lives. I encourage you to stay open to the mystery of it all.

Always remember that it's possible for health issues, limiting beliefs, and ingrained painful emotions to be substantially weakened or completely released in an instant, catapulting you into a healthier, more joyful way of being. Just don't expect it.

Let me share a story with you about an unexpected and sudden healing. In 2020, during the COVID-19 pandemic, a series of extremely stressful events occurred in my universe. My dad had two strokes, and my mum was struggling with her mobility. For many reasons I was extremely concerned about them. They both lived alone in the UK: one in Cornwall and the other in Yorkshire. For many months, they barely saw a soul. Due to the COVID restrictions at the time, my brother, who lives in Wales, wasn't permitted to cross into England to visit either of them, and I wasn't able to travel to the UK to be with them either. My parents were isolated and struggling, and because of the outbreak, I truly didn't know if I would ever see them again. Added to that, in the first month of the lockdown, we had to put our beautiful beagle, Ruby, to sleep. That broke our hearts into tiny fragments.

And unbelievably, I had three cancer scares at the same time as all this was going on: breast, retina, and skin. Additional testing was performed, and the medical professionals were saying things that made me very stressed. I had Mohs surgery to remove skin cancer from my face.

I was concerned about my daughter and son, aged twenty-three and twenty-one at the time, choosing to remain in Brooklyn and Boston, respectively. During all the panic and fear, the adult offspring of virtually all my friends returned home to be with their parents. Even though I was very proud of them for handling it so well, I was also extremely nervous because they were out on the streets at night, protesting in support of Black Lives Matter.

Many of us had a ridiculously tough time during the COVID pandemic. Many people had far worse experiences than I did. Nevertheless, my levels of anxiety and stress reached alarming levels during that time, and they impacted my life in bizarre and unexpected ways. For starters, I'd become terrified of narrow roads. Roadworks with concrete barriers were the worst for me.

When I visited the UK in 2021, I discovered that British country roads — especially the ridiculously narrow ones, the width of a human hair — winding their way through the countryside in a curvaceous fashion with only occasional passing places, were a source of great distress for me. They set me off big time. These ancient roads, known as "sunken lanes," lie several feet lower than the surrounding fields, worn down and compacted over centuries by the passage of carts, animals, and foot traffic. Driving through tunnels petrified me too. I drove close to the lane divider, keeping as far away from the tunnel walls as possible. There I was: panic pumping through my veins, a white-knuckle death grip on the steering wheel, crawling along at a snail's pace with impatient drivers honking at me left, right, and center. It was genuinely terrifying.

Tall escalators also caused me tremendous trouble. I would shake with fear, my heart rate going bonkers, and the only way to reach the top was to crouch down as I rode on them. This was very embarrassing, so I avoided them and used elevators whenever possible! All in all, I had quite a problem on my hands.

In 2022, persistent and painful hip and back issues prompted me to seek ways to heal and find relief.

I'd heard from Deb, a trusted friend, that Rolfing was an effective way to release the energetics of injuries and emotional trauma from the body, helping it return to harmonious balance. Rolfing is a bodywork technique that realigns the body's structure by working with connective tissues, improving posture, and releasing tension. Deb recommended an excellent Rolfer, Sharon Sklar, who seemed like a perfect fit, so I signed up for Sharon's Rolfing Ten Series.

I didn't mention these intense fears about driving and escalators when I met Sharon. I focused on my hip and back issues. However, to my utter astonishment, after the second session, as I drove home through a tunnel and roadworks with narrow lanes lined by concrete barriers, I noticed that my hands were relaxed on the steering wheel, and my heart rate was barely elevated. My body felt about 80 percent less tense, and I remained calm. It was a gigantic welcome shift! After a couple of weeks, my driving returned to normal.

The escalator problem also resolved itself. In Milan airport, riding an escalator while holding onto two suitcases, I said to myself, *I've been on here a while; this must be a tall escalator.* And I felt totally relaxed. At the top, James asked me if I was okay. I was confused and wondered why he'd asked. *Why wouldn't I be?* Then I realized what had just happened. I'd come up a tall escalator, not even holding on, and felt completely fine!

Those fears about driving and the intense anxiety vanished from just a few Rolfing sessions, and I hadn't even told Sharon about them. What a relief!

My Rolfing story illustrates how our emotional, mental, physical, and spiritual selves are interrelated. It's impossible to separate them. You may have heard about how our thoughts, beliefs, and emotions significantly affect our health issues. The late Louise Hay detailed the thoughts and feelings that can contribute to specific health problems. For example, Hay believed that adrenal problems may be associated with defeatism, no longer caring for the self, anxiety, alcoholism, feelings of futility, guilt, inadequacy, and self-rejection.

When I have something going on with my body, I often look up the suggested dynamics for that issue to understand what might be contributing to the imbalance. This can be helpful, bringing our attention to something that may need assistance. But I also believe it's more important to trust what our body tells us rather than mindlessly following a generalized model. We're the experts on ourselves. So, it's valuable to check in with our own body's wisdom, asking if those elements are contributing to our situation, and if not, what is. Other great questions to ask our body are: *What are you trying to tell me?*; *What is the energetic cause of this health issue?*; or *Are there steps you'd like me to take to help us return to a healthy balance?*

Expectations and attachment to outcomes often create considerable problems for us on our healing path. When things aren't going how we'd like, we can feel angry, frustrated, impatient, and hopeless. It can be challenging to let go of trying to control the process. After all, wanting to heal and improve our lives is only natural. Healing often has its own beautiful way of unfolding, in its own sweet timing. If expectations get in your way about what healing will look or feel like, how or when it will occur, or if you have an attachment to a specific outcome, please be gentle and kind to yourself. Do your best to let go of them and be curious, open-minded, patient, and accepting of what is. Your life will then flow more freely, with greater ease and harmony.

In the past, I've given away my power to some healers, believing them to be the authority figures and that their intuitive hits were better than mine. Doing this weakens the connection to our intuition and the Divine, and self-doubt often creeps in. So, I urge you to trust your intuition over what anyone else tells you. Work with those who encourage you to stay in your power, guiding you to tap into your intuition and to deepen your relationship with the Divine. It's also wise to work with those who are free of judgment and personal agendas, and who continue to do their inner healing work. Lastly, just because some practitioners charge very high fees doesn't necessarily make them great.

In a nutshell, be discerning about who you choose to work with. Trust your gut, and if it resonates, use the suggested approaches in the "Alchemy Tools" section at the end of the book to help you determine who is a good fit for you.

Sometimes, the healing path can feel lonely, extremely intense, scary, or exhausting. We may find ourselves in the tricky waters of calling ourselves out on our beliefs, patterns, and strategies, taking responsibility for the part we've played in our painful situations and peeling away layers of trauma and difficult emotions. It can be hard to handle regular life, feeling fragile and more sensitive than before. I know that challenging place well.

Times like these are simply part of the healing journey. To support ourselves in moving through these transformations, it is helpful to take some deep, slow breaths and spend time in silence. Take yourself into the core of your heart, offering yourself tremendous amounts of gentleness and compassion. Epsom salt baths and being in nature also boost the energetic clearings.

Spending time each day doing something that we enjoy, that makes us smile or laugh, also makes these times a little easier. As we look after ourselves, loving and nurturing ourselves, we raise our vibration, which helps us to heal on every level of our being.

Freedom and self-love are always available to us when we turn our attention to what lies deeper than our painful patterns, intense emotions, and negative thoughts. It takes just a moment to take our awareness deep inside, and when we do, we experience peace and reconnect with our true nature, as *Love*.

Throughout the healing process, tending to ourselves lovingly, with compassion and patience for those parts of us that are suffering, is essential. As we peel away layers of emotions, we gradually reveal more and more of our beautiful, radiant hearts, making it easier to tap into self-love and stay there, creating more peace and harmony in our lives.

Hand on heart, my life has improved in the most beautiful and incredible ways. I'm much more peaceful, compassionate, and loving these days. My heart has opened, limiting beliefs have vanished, and I truly love myself. I'm profoundly grateful for all the healing that has occurred and for the gifts that emanated from every single difficulty.

Sometimes it can take a while for these gifts to come into our awareness, but let me reassure you that even in the darkest of times, they are there, waiting for us to receive them.

# 5

# ON THE WINGS OF A DRAGONFLY

The road to forgiveness can be lengthy and convoluted. It can be tough to forgive ourselves and others for things that have happened. In my personal experience and that of my clients, some form of healing is often necessary before true forgiveness can flow. Over the years, I've discovered one of the greatest gifts that genuine forgiveness can shower on us is that as we forgive, we release ourselves from painful memories and a place of victimhood, blame, and suffering. In the act of forgiveness, we truly set ourselves free from it all.

I've been surprised to find that there were times when I was able to forgive myself or others, before I could fully accept the situation and surrender to a power greater than myself. This seemed counterintuitive as my logical mind assumed that acceptance and surrender would always be prerequisites to forgiveness. At other times, I've opened to beautiful acceptance and surrender, yet complete forgiveness was much slower to come to the party. What I can be sure of is that there seems to be no formula. It's an unpredictable, living, breathing thing, and it's best to go with the flow without trying to force it.

In April 2020, in the early days of the COVID lockdown, I sat trembling in a treatment chair at my dermatologist's office, my face having been numbed in preparation for surgery. I was breathing deeply and slowly to calm my racing heart. I was petrified. A plastic surgeon was about to surgically remove a squamous cell carcinoma via Mohs procedure from just under the bottom corner of my nose. If you're unfamiliar with a Mohs procedure, let me share what happens. The surgeon cuts tissue away from the area of the carcinoma; the sample is quickly taken down the corridor to a lab technician, who tests the excised tissue to check if the surgeon has removed all the cancerous cells. If not, they continue taking more flesh until the area is completely clear. If required, they perform a skin graft, and then the surgeon stitches you up.

At the time of the cancer diagnosis, I was flailing around in excruciating grief from the recent death of our beloved beagle, Ruby. The heavy grief, combined with my two other cancer concerns, and constant worry for my parents in the UK, was almost unbearable. On top of it all, both my daughter and son had chosen to stay in Brooklyn and Boston, which added to my anxieties during that unpredictable, uncertain time.

Ruby, almost twelve years old, had been in horrendous pain after hurting her back by jumping up on the sofa, and the vet couldn't get her comfortable with pain medications.

I hated to admit it, but we were out of options, and we had to make the heart-wrenching decision to put her to sleep. Within days after her death, a strange lump appeared out of nowhere on my face. At first, I thought it was a pimple, but it didn't go down, and then I thought it looked like a wart. James suggested that I get it checked out. My dermatologist wasn't seeing patients in person due to COVID. The offices were closed other than for surgical emergencies, so she asked me to send her photos. When she saw the images, she sent me off for a biopsy. The doctor who conducted the biopsy was convinced the growth was a wart. He told me not to worry and assured me he was sending off the lump for a biopsy just to give me peace of mind.

He asked me if I had a dog. I told him I didn't; it was easier for me that way. Ruby had just died, and I was raw with grief. I didn't fancy bursting into tears in his office. He was most confused by this because it was such a strange place to develop a wart unless I'd picked it up from a dog. I didn't enlighten him.

A light went on in my mind. I recalled that in the last few days of Ruby's life, I'd spent hours hugging her, holding her, and burying my face in her fur. I cried so hard into her fur that I thought my heart would shatter into tiny pieces. I wasn't ready for her to go. I had such a deep bond with her, which had only developed after she'd stopped being such a destructive, escape-artist rascal as a young dog. I adored her willful, naughty, untrainable, independent, loving, outrageously intelligent self.

A couple of years before Ruby's death, I'd been aware

of small lumps on her skin and had asked the vet about them. He didn't share what they were but said they were nothing to worry about. After my conversation with the dermatologist, I deduced that I'd picked up a wart from her during the last couple of weeks of her life. When the biopsy result came back as a squamous cell carcinoma, I was shell-shocked, devastated, and furious, as the dermatologist had been adamant that my lump wasn't cancerous. I'd even been joking with my nearest and dearest that I'd had a near miss and that it was just a wart from our beloved Ruby.

My doctor recommended that I get it removed with great haste and pulled strings to get me on the plastic surgeon's schedule as soon as possible. So, that's how I'd ended up sitting in the treatment chair, terrified, as he approached my face with his scalpel.

I considered myself lucky as it took only one extraction for them to be certain they had taken the cancerous cells out. I was extremely relieved that further tissue didn't have to be removed from my face and that no skin grafts were needed. Before the surgeon stitched me up, he told me he was using dissolvable stitches because, due to COVID, he wasn't seeing patients for follow-up appointments to remove stitches. I was very concerned and apprehensive that dissolvable stitches would leave a more noticeable scar on my face, but he reassured me that it would be fine and would leave the same degree of scarring as stitches comprised of surgical threads. I trusted him.

All stitched up, I was in shock and shaking when I left

the dermatologist's office; even my bones were trembling. I was very wobbly as I slowly descended the stairs into the reception area. I felt spacey and disoriented as I left the building. James wasn't allowed into their offices due to COVID protocols, so he was waiting in the car at the entrance. I opened the car door, climbed in, and immediately pulled the sun visor down to look in the mirror. The lump on my face had been very small, so I assumed the incision would be minimal. I was absolutely devastated when I saw myself. It turned out he'd cut me all the way from the bottom of my nose to my lip, my face was severely swollen, and I looked horrendous. Tears of pity poured down my cheeks.

In the days that followed, I felt as though I'd been violated. And to my horror, some of the stitches dissolved too quickly and didn't seem to be holding the wound in place properly. I panicked that I would be left with a worse scar than necessary and called for advice, but the plastic surgeon said it was fine and refused to see me. I was incandescently furious with him. The wound didn't heal very well, and it left a big, red, lumpy scar. I was so angry and upset with him. I kept ranting internally that he'd done a terrible job and that he'd diminished my beauty, and I couldn't snap out of my toxic self-talk.

Every time I looked in the mirror, I was stung by intense sorrow and grief. I avoided mirrors as much as possible, and on the occasions when I accidentally caught a glimpse of myself, I chose to look into my eyes instead of staring at my wound. Friends wanted to visit to show their support and love, but I hated seeing them. I detected pity on their faces as they looked at me and sensed they were relieved that it wasn't their face that had been scarred.

The upside of wearing masks in public during the pandemic was that they hid my scar beautifully! When I was out and about, no one knew it was there. I could be me again — Rachel before the surgery, as if it had never happened. I was incredibly grateful for those masks.

Overflowing with self-criticism for not taking more time to think through my options before surgery and beating myself up for not asking around to find a brilliant plastic surgeon, I kept thinking, *If only I'd done things differently; if only I'd made better decisions.* I felt that I'd let myself down and betrayed myself by not speaking up and insisting that he put proper stitches in my face to minimize scarring. Even though, most likely, he would have refused. He wouldn't even see me when I was worried about the stitches dissolving too quickly and my wound coming apart. I was distraught for a long while.

When the offices of my original dermatologist reopened, I couldn't face going back to them for skin checks, so I switched to a new dermatologist in a different practice who was highly recommended. When she saw my scar, she was very troubled by the surgeon's work and disapproved of his choice of stitching material.

I considered having more surgery to try and fix what he'd done to me, so I made an appointment to see a highly recommended plastic surgeon. He advised me not to bother. He didn't feel the possible minor improvement would be worth the trauma of further surgery and the associated long period of healing. He said that the skin had been pulled so tight during the last surgery that it would be tough to re-stitch it, and there was a risk of more nerve damage on my face. There was a distinct possibility that it might look even worse than it did now. It was at that moment that I realized I was going to have to accept what had happened and how I looked post-surgery.

I felt such a powerful sense of injustice; it burned like a fire. I was incandescently angry with the plastic surgeon and with myself for making a series of bad decisions. The self-destructive story kept circling round and round in my head; it was a dizzying mix of misery and suffering.

I'll be honest: it took me a long time to come to terms with the way my face looked. To boot, I'd even been beating myself up about how horrified I was at the depths of my vanity, that it bothered me so much when far worse things were going on in the world. But I just couldn't shake it off. None of my attempts at re-framing made it seem okay, no matter how creative I was. Countless energy-healing sessions and ceremonies were conducted to help me heal from the mental, emotional, and physical trauma of that experience. I used scar-reducing creams, had laser therapy, and sent so much love to myself.

It came to me in meditation that the reason this experience had hit me so hard was because it had triggered old childhood wounds about not being able to trust anyone, that no one looks after me, and that the world isn't a safe place. Those powerful beliefs came from those two horrendous accidents in my early childhood — losing the end of my finger and the nasty burns to my face that happened when my mum was supposed to be taking care of me, making sure I didn't get in harm's way.

This surgery experience had been difficult to release because, deep inside, my inner child was struggling and suffering. She had experienced horrific, traumatizing accidents and was distraught at how it was possible they could have happened. *Wasn't my mum supposed to keep me safe?*

I focused on connecting with my inner child and helped her feel better by sending her love and tenderness. I let her know that I'm always here for her, looking after her, and keeping her safe.

Sessions with a therapist trained in Eye Movement Desensitization and Reprocessing (EMDR) played a significant role in helping me to completely accept what happened.

As my younger self felt progressively safer and well looked after, I finally found that I could forgive the plastic surgeon. In forgiving him, I set myself free, which rolled over into truly forgiving myself for my response to what had taken place. I was then able to see that we'd been in the middle of a crazy time in history, and the surgeon was doing his best under challenging circumstances. Stress and fear were rampant in our society, and we were all trying to protect ourselves. I let both of us off the hook. Yes, in normal times, I would have sought a second opinion and taken the time to select an excellent plastic surgeon — I knew that. I realized I made the best decision I could during that difficult and anxious situation. Holding onto the suffering and blame had been emotionally damaging and exhausting for me. All was forgiven; what a relief.

My scar has become part of my beauty instead of taking away from it. It adds character to my face, tells a story, and adds to the richness of my life. It reminds me of my intense and profound love for my precious dog Ruby and hers for me. The scar on my face is a tattoo, a memory of her. I wear her with love and remembrance.

In my experience and that of many of my clients, sometimes it can take a while before we're able to forgive others and ourselves for things that were said, not said, done, and not done. As I've already mentioned, I had to undergo a considerable amount of emotional and mental healing before I was even close to being able to forgive those who I believed had caused a great deal of upset and misery in my life, especially my parents.

Peeling away layers of painful, trapped emotions, clearing the effects of traumatic events, and dissolving heaps of unhelpful beliefs about myself and others were necessary for me to be ready to open into forgiveness. And in the case of one or two people from my past, no matter what I tried to do to heal the situation, I couldn't seem to let go of my angst with them. I was stuck in a stubborn cycle of resistance and couldn't break out of it. In those cases, it just took longer than I would have liked. It was exasperating that it took so long, but I came to realize that more things needed to happen, and deeper insights were necessary before forgiveness could occur. If you can relate to that, if forgiveness is difficult or slow-moving, please be gentle and patient with yourself. It often eases the way when we can let go of our expectations around forgiveness and refuse to believe any self-judgment or self-criticism about why it's so hard, why it's taking so long, or that we'll never be able to forgive them. Forgive yourself for not being able to forgive!

When people have done horrendous things, it can seem impossible to be able and willing to forgive them. We may get stuck in victimhood, believing ourselves wronged — hanging out in a place of powerlessness and blaming others for how we feel and the circumstances we find ourselves in. A wide range of intense emotions can run riot in our systems. Sometimes, those persistent emotions won't leave us alone, weakening our ability to feel calm and loving, keeping well-being just out of arm's reach. The truth is, when we don't forgive others, and we're glued tenaciously to victimhood and blame, we're the ones who suffer. We tie ourselves up in knots in a complicated cocktail of energetic, emotional, and mental threads, which can feel disempowering, exhausting, and hopeless. Lack of forgiveness tends to keep us captive in old patterns, stuck in the past with a sinking feeling of no end in sight to how we're feeling. In these situations, moving on with our lives can be like wading through molasses.

Please understand that I'm not saying it's okay for people to treat us however they want. By forgiving them, we're not saying they aren't responsible for their actions or that we're enabling them to do it all over again, leaving ourselves vulnerable to future issues. Forgiving someone doesn't let them off the hook for how they behaved, and it doesn't condone their actions or permit them to repeat their behavior.

We often need to enforce clear, healthy boundaries with those we've had difficulties with, sending them strong messages that we are standing up for ourselves, putting our needs first, and refusing to let the old behaviors continue.

When we forgive another, our heart space opens, and we release ourselves from any hold we felt they had over us and/or the events that took place.

As we forgive, we free ourselves from the past and step back into the present moment and into our innate power. From there, we can open to the potential for self-healing in powerful and lasting ways, bolstering our ability to love ourselves.

In the highly charged emotional days following our dad's unexpected and sudden death, John and I were deep in the process of selecting his coffin, choosing flowers, making arrangements to sit with him at the funeral director's chapel of rest, and planning his cremation and a celebration-of-life gathering. As I worked my way through the long list of tasks to be completed, I heard my guides encouraging me to write a letter of forgiveness to my dad that would go into the cremation furnace with him.

When I heard their beloved guidance, I immediately felt drawn to do as they suggested. I wanted to write the letter on something that made my heart sing, so I nipped into town and came across some beautiful, heavy-weight writing paper with a single graceful dragonfly embossed on each page, with matching envelopes. As soon as my eyes fell upon it in the store, I knew in my heart that it would be perfect for my task. I sensed and trusted that my guides would tell me when the time was right for the letter to be written. Used to their ways, I was relaxed about not knowing when that would happen and felt content that I was prepared for when the words began to flow.

I knew our departure date was rapidly approaching, but I didn't want to force or push the letter writing. I continued to trust that my guides knew what they were up to. The day before our flight to the UK, the moment finally came when the words were ready to emerge onto the page. Taking plenty of deep breaths and drinking plenty of water, I connected with my guides and wrote out what they shared with me. What tumbled out onto the paper was a loving, compassionate, and gentle letter where I forgave myself and my dad for our troubled, complicated relationship and how we had both shown up and behaved through all those years. And I set us both free. I shared that I'd wished we'd been able to have a wonderful, close relationship and that I was sorry we had never managed that. I sent him off with love in my heart and wished him well. My heart poured out onto the paper in an exquisitely concise, powerful, and beautiful manner. As I read it out loud, I could feel the incredible energy that weaved its way through my words.

My letter flew with me to the UK, and it traveled down to Cornwall in a rental car. When we went to sit with my dad's body in the funeral director's chapel of rest, the day before his cremation, I placed it carefully on top of his coffin, tucked in amongst the gorgeous, colorful floral display that I'd chosen for his send-off.

Unfortunately, James tested positive for COVID that night and felt extremely unwell. Poor guy, he felt terrible about the timing and that it meant he would miss the cremation gathering. Despite the risk of infection, John, my sister-in-law Teresa, and I still wanted to be together at the time of the cremation. We opted to be outside on the Prince Charles Pier in Falmouth, a place where we'd all spent time with dad, devouring delicious ice creams and having lunch in a local café as we looked out at the picturesque harbor.

As requested, the funeral director had placed the letter into the coffin with Dad, and they entered the fire together.

At the actual time of his cremation, the three of us huddled together on the pier on a drizzly, cold December morning. With raindrops gently kissing my face, I whispered the words from my letter, so quietly that only I could hear. I sent him off into the fire with love and absolute forgiveness, a gift to both of us that was far greater than any words could ever describe. I felt the magnitude of my act of forgiveness in every cell of my being. It had a power greater than anything I'd ever experienced before. Something had been unleashed within me.

If you've had tumultuous relationships with a close relative in your life, and you get the chance to do something similar when they die, I highly recommend it as a loving gift to you both — one that will assist with healing the relationship at the end of their earthly life and set you both free. On the other hand, if the person you had those difficulties with has already died, please know that you haven't missed your opportunity. It's still incredibly powerful to write a forgiveness letter long after they've departed.

Write the letter from your heart, coming from a place of love and compassion, and create your own sacred ceremony. You may know exactly what you would like to do and what feels most fitting. If you're looking for some inspiration, perhaps you could get quiet and still, bring the person to mind, read the letter out loud or silently, and fall into your heart space. When you're ready, set light to your letter outside, in a responsible manner, in a fireplace, firepit, or a cauldron — my personal favorite — imagining it burning with them, all the difficulties and painful memories returning to the Universe. It's all energy. Through this act, you are setting yourself free, unshackling your energy so you can move on and embrace the present.

There have been times when I thought I'd forgiven myself or others, but then I'd get triggered again. On closer inspection, I realized that I'd barely scratched the surface of the amount of forgiveness that was possible. On reflection, this seemed to be an invitation to allow even deeper levels of forgiveness to occur. The reality is that sometimes we need to forgive incrementally rather than going for 100 percent.

It can be extremely difficult, verging on impossible, to forgive someone or yourself completely on the first go. So, go easy on yourself and let your expectations of that happening fall between your fingers. Maybe it will happen; maybe it won't. Instead of it being a moment of despair, just forgive to whatever degree is achievable for you at that moment. Then, over time, you can revisit the issue and continue to open into more forgiveness if or when it becomes available.

When you're calm, still, and centered, bring to mind the issue and ask yourself how much you're ready to forgive right now. Then, simply wait to hear, see, or know what percentage of forgiveness is ready to be experienced. It can be anything from 0 to 100 percent. Whatever response you get, be enormously grateful to yourself, take some deep breaths, relax, let any resistance melt away, and allow the forgiveness process to unfold.

If you're keen to dive even deeper, you can also ask if anything else is needed for additional forgiveness to take place. Listen to any guidance you receive with an open heart, and take action if you feel called to do so. You may find that this unlocks greater forgiveness.

In my forties, I finally spoke with my mum about her leaving home when I was a child. At the time, she was staying with us for a couple of weeks in Charlotte, North Carolina. One day, a strong urge suddenly arose in me to openly and honestly discuss with her what had happened when I was young.

As a child, I remember deciding I'd protect her feelings by never letting her discover how much her departure had affected me. I didn't want her to know that I'd felt unsafe and neglected, and had spent much of my life struggling with deep-rooted beliefs of unlovability and unworthiness. Together with fears of abandonment and intimacy, the heady mix had made it difficult for me to have healthy relationships of any kind.

We were sitting in my family room that day when I began to calmly ask her questions about why she had left and shared with her how it had impacted me.

It was a powerful testament to the healing transformations and forgiveness that had occurred within me, that I was able to have that awkward conversation without blaming or judging her. There was no anger or sadness. Not a single tear flowed. Dry-eyed, my words came from a powerful, loving place inside me, with profound compassion for both of us.

At one point, she remarked that I must hate her for what she did. I replied that I didn't and shared that I'd completely forgiven her for what happened back then. I listened with an open heart and mind as she answered my questions, and I came to understand that her own sense of unworthiness played a massive role in why she made those decisions. She apologized for what she'd done and said she'd always thought she would say sorry to me on her deathbed. I laughed and said kindly, "That would have been a bit dramatic! It's better that you're doing it now. I mean, I live in America and it's very likely I'll miss that moment."

Although it was an extremely uncomfortable conversation, I could feel the immense healing power of forgiveness present in the room that day. Our conversation cleared the air between us. The elephant in the room had departed. It cleared the way for a better, healthier relationship between us. These days, I genuinely enjoy and appreciate her company. It was a blessed healing, for sure.

Forgiving ourselves is just as important as forgiving other people. If we have a habit of being hard on ourselves by judging and criticizing our thoughts, emotions, and actions, self-forgiveness can be especially hard to come by. It can be easier to forgive others than ourselves. Do you harshly criticize yourself, punishing yourself for both minor and major mistakes?

Oh my! I wrestled with that pattern for many years and was incredibly harsh with myself. And that made it outrageously challenging to forgive myself for some of my decisions and actions. Whether the events were huge with massive, long-term consequences or relatively minor, they all created a lot of toxic self-criticism and self-judgment within my system, along the lines of *I should have known better; I made a terrible decision; I didn't take enough care; I'm so stupid! Why did I do that?*; or *I've gone and done it now!*

I felt a great deal of compassion towards myself when I realized that this harmful pattern was created in my childhood and came from witnessing my parents' behavior. As young children, we soak it all in without question; it's the way life is, the norm, and it can easily become part of our personality and coping strategies.

With profound thanks to my spiritual teacher, Gangaji, I've come to realize that we have a choice when the urge to respond in this poisonous fashion arises. Rather than letting the same old pattern run riot, we can interrupt it by meeting, loving, and embracing it — staying still in the eye of the storm, refusing to believe our toxic thoughts, and opening to the energies that flood our bodies. Yes, it requires immense commitment, strength, and courage to stay motionless amid the commotion. But when we do so, without acting out of dense, heavy emotions, we begin to loosen the grip that destructive pattern has on us, reducing its power and rendering it less able to hijack us and cause immense suffering in our lives.

As we shift the ingrained pattern of self-judgment and self-criticism and heal the unworthiness at its core, we increase our capacity to be more loving and forgiving towards ourselves. Our ability to love ourselves grows as we forgive ourselves for everything we have and haven't done.

Thankfully, tremendous progress has been made in shifting my old tendency to berate myself. Last year, I sent for an elegant wrap with an interesting woven texture. The day it arrived, I'd been painting up a storm in my studio.

I opened the box excitedly, admiring the gorgeous wrap as I threw it over me with delight. *Yes!! I love it! That's a keeper!* I popped it into a drawer in my closet. A couple of days later, I was getting ready to go out for dinner with a dear friend. I put on my new wrap, and a flash of bright yellow caught my eye. On closer inspection, I discovered a splodge of yellow oil paint on the front edge. *Hmmm.*

Now, in the past, that would have set me off on a torrent of self-hatred and abuse. In sharp contrast to that madness, I felt relaxed. I took it to the laundry room and tried a few stain-removing tricks, but my attempts didn't make much of a difference. A wonderful thought entered my mind: *This is the wrap of a passionate artist who loves to throw oil paint around!* It was like I'd sewn my name tag into it. I smiled at how the yellow stain was a reminder of my creativity and a celebration of how my paintings contribute beauty to the world.

During her eleven years of exuberant life, my adorable, willful, highly intelligent beagle, Ruby Linnett, damaged many of our possessions and caused general mayhem. Deep gouges appeared on the dining room table and chairs. She chewed rugs, left nasty stains on the sofa and carpet, and threw up on the breakfast table, her acidic vomit permanently bleaching the wood. Ruby chewed a hole in the wicker umbrella stand while lizard hunting. She loved emptying the contents of the kitchen bin all over the floor, scratching the kitchen cabinetry in the process. During her life, she went to impressive lengths to reach food left on the kitchen island or the stovetop. I could fill a book on Ruby stories alone!

I was very relieved when she finally started to calm down and stopped being so destructive at around seven years of age.

In the last year of her life, a vet recommended switching her to raw food to help with her stomach issues. It didn't work, but she instantly became feral. We'd recently replaced the breakfast table. Tired of the vomit stain and scratches, we'd purchased a beautiful round wooden table, confident that Ruby's crazy days were over.

Believing it to be safe, one night after dinner with friends, I left the remains of our meal on the kitchen island — a lamb chop on a plate and some mashed sweet potato in a serving bowl. I pushed the chairs close against our lovely, new, unblemished table, and we nipped out for sundowners at the beach.

On our return, the bowl had been licked clean, and the lamb chop was gone. My eyes moved to our new table. To my horror, the table had massive, deep gouge marks. It looked like she'd been slipping off with her hind legs and hanging on for dear life with her front paws! We didn't even leave any food on the table! I can only assume she'd been licking the wood, hoping to catch some delicious flavors. I was so cross with her. Good grief, we'd only just had the table delivered!

That marked the end of the raw food experiment. After returning to a non-raw diet, Ruby calmed down within a few days and reverted to her well-behaved senior self.

My fury subsided over the next week, and I forgave her. In the past, I'd struggled to forgive myself or others when things got damaged, so I was pleased by my progress, even though I'd still reacted.

Less than a year after the table incident, we had to put our beloved Ruby to sleep. I'm so relieved that forgiveness flooded in before she died. She left her signature behind. These days, I love running my fingers over those canyons. They make me smile and remind me of our loving, determined furry friend.

Forgiveness is often accompanied by plenty of tears, and a profound sense of relief tends to descend, imbued with love and gentleness.

Life presents us with plenty of opportunities to forgive. Sometimes, all that's required is giving ourselves permission and reassuring ourselves that it's safe to do so.

Forgiveness is a tremendous gift to ourselves and to the world at large. It opens the doorway to releasing wounds from our painful pasts and sets us free.

It serves us well to remember that forgiveness doesn't

rely on anyone else taking any action. It doesn't wait for an apology for another's behavior or for them to forgive us for anything we have done. The truth is that we always hold the power and ability to forgive.

As we forgive ourselves and others, the capacity to truly love and accept all aspects of our being increases exponentially.

# 6

# WHEN ENOUGH IS ENOUGH

Having healthy boundaries is an essential part of treating ourselves with love, respect, and compassion. However, it can be exceedingly challenging to live our lives with clear, supportive boundaries, especially when we've had a dysfunctional upbringing and experienced trauma. Although I've cleaned up many of my boundary issues, poor boundaries still trip me up and present me with the toughest challenges.

People-pleasing is often one of the major patterns at play when we have boundary issues. In people-pleasing mode, we prioritize the needs of others above our own, even to our detriment. We go out of our way to please another and to avoid rocking the boat, believing — often unconsciously — that it will keep us safe somehow. So, at its root, people-pleasing is often a survival strategy. The intention behind it can follow the energetic thread of *If I please you, then you'll love me, accept me, keep me safe, protect me, or take care of me.* It's usually an attempt to avoid rejection, abandonment, isolation, being the cause of someone's fury, or being the target of their outburst.

Cultural conditioning can contribute to the formation of people-pleasing habits. I grew up in an English working-class environment, which was rife with unhealthy relationship dynamics. Men were typically regarded as the authority figures; they held the power and were put on a pedestal. Women deferred to them and often resented them while doing their best to avoid angering the men. Women often waited hand-and-foot on men while paying little attention to their own needs. I soaked all of this in and believed it was just how life was.

People-pleasing often creates unhealthy, dysfunctional relationships. In pleasing mode, we tend to do things we don't feel good about. Over time, this can generate tremendous inner resentment, anger and frustration, and sometimes, even humiliation and shame. A sense of self-betrayal and hopelessness can run deep. It's very tough to love yourself when this powerful pattern is operating.

I strongly suspect that my own pleasing tendencies arose from my dad paying me little attention, being emotionally unavailable, and having a bad temper. When I was young, I was keen to please him to prevent an outburst. I wanted him to accept, love, and look after me.

It also showed up with my mum. I tried to protect her by hiding the emotional damage I'd experienced growing up. I attempted to minimize her upset and guilt by telling her I was fine when I wasn't. I carried the weight of my hurt, so she didn't have to. I believed she wasn't strong enough to cope with the truth.

Thankfully, the further I've traveled on my healing path, the fewer people I try to please.

I'm curious: Do you have people you try to please in

your life? If so, who are they? And do you know where the dynamic originates from?

Let me share a story with you that demonstrates my people-pleasing tendency. Perhaps you'll recognize yourself in some way.

In May 2023, I was in Santa Fe, New Mexico, with James. We were supposed to be in South Africa on a greatly anticipated vacation, but due to circumstances beyond our control, we'd been forced to cancel on the day of departure. In a state of tremendous disappointment and desperate to go somewhere, we booked a last-minute trip to Santa Fe. We were staying in a hotel outside of town, in a gorgeous, quiet spot that was absolutely pitch black at night.

We were having a brilliant time, enjoying great food, hiking, spa treatments, and seeing dear friends. On the third night, in the complete inky black darkness of our hotel room, I got up to go to the bathroom. As I hurried back to bed, keen to hop back into the warmth and coziness, I smacked my right foot against the corner of the heavy, rustic wooden bedpost. Now, I've stubbed my toe many times, and it hurts, but this was a whole new level of agony. I shouted out in excruciating pain, and a stream of colorful profanities flew out of my mouth! Trained in Reiki, I put my healing hands on my foot and finally drifted off to sleep, hoping for the best. The next day, when I got up and put weight on my foot, it was exceedingly sore. I strongly suspected that my toe or foot was broken.

As I could barely walk, we had to modify our plans for the rest of the trip. I bought a walking cane and borrowed some wide, cushioned HOKA® athletic slide sandals from my beloved friend, JJ, because my swollen foot didn't fit into my shoes. I was forced to use the hotel buggy service to get about. I'm usually such an active person, and it was frustrating and embarrassing being unable to move under my own steam.

The Universe was offering me an opportunity for personal growth in a challenging area: asking for and receiving help when I needed it. An abundance of assistance came my way, and people were so caring and thoughtful about my injury and lack of mobility. The buggy rides ended up being delightful. One of my friendly drivers piped up with, "You should consider yourself lucky; in the old days, they'd have cut your foot off!" Cute.

A precious gem lay awaiting my discovery in the aftermath of my mishap. I'd been feeling fed up because we'd had to cancel our South African vacation, and on our consolation trip, I'd damaged my foot and was virtually immobile. I'll admit to you that I was feeling upset and exasperated, wondering what the heck the Universe was up to.

My wise, spiritual friend, Kim, emailed me the morning after my accident with great suggestions on hikes James and I could take through the dramatic landscape near Taos. In my reply, I told her about my toe injury and explained that the hiking trip to Taos was now outside the realms of possibility. I quipped, "I'm not sure what the Universe is trying to tell me."

She quickly responded, "Perhaps the Universe is telling you to put the light on!"

On the one hand, it made me laugh, but her words went much deeper, and a profound realization came into my awareness. When I asked myself why I hadn't turned the light on, it dawned on me that I never switch the light on in the night, to avoid disturbing James.

Even when it was pitch black and I couldn't see anything, I still put his slumber needs before my own safety.

On retelling the story to a friend, she remarked, "I bet he woke up when you broke your toe!" He certainly did with all the commotion. My attempt to avoid rousing him had failed. It was time for me to make some changes and prioritize my needs.

Bizarrely, a few days before our holiday, I'd been guided to buy a tiny but extremely bright travel torch at the hardware store. I dug it out of my luggage and used it for the rest of our trip. James muttered it was very bright and was disturbing him. I emphatically told him it was tough nuts; my safety was more important than his sleep quality. When I returned home, I softened; it wasn't his fault that I kept putting his needs first to my detriment. I didn't need to take it out on him with a bright strobe light that could be seen from space! So, I found a great compromise: motion detector lights with a soft, soothing orange glow. Win-win.

An X-ray confirmed a broken toe. The Universe had shown me rather loudly the consequences of my people-pleasing pattern, one so deeply ingrained that it took breaking a bone to force me to stop in my tracks and make changes. The message came loud and clear: *Stop putting everyone else first! Your needs are just as important as everyone else's.*

Perhaps you can reflect on ways in which you prioritize the needs of others and disregard your own. What does that evoke in you? Are there some positive changes you're willing to make?

An essential part of having healthy boundaries and, therefore, loving ourselves, is responding to requests from others with confidence and kindness based on what we truly desire. It can be challenging to say "no" to what we don't want and hard to ask for what we truly desire. I love Byron Katie's words: "To say no is to say yes to yourself."

Although it might be tricky at first, learning that it's safe to say "no," that sometimes we need to say "no," and to speak up when we're not okay with things are essential skills to develop for our own self-care.

We can find ourselves worried about the reaction of others when we say "no" to their requests or suggestions. Feeling uncomfortable about it is okay, but don't let it stop you from speaking up. If your "no" is met with a negative reaction from others, treat it as an opportunity for personal growth. Lean into any discomfort about their response and how they might feel about you, breathe deeply, and connect with the courageous part of yourself — we all have one. Be true to yourself and refuse to give in, even if they try to convince you otherwise.

Saying "yes" when we'd rather say "no" often ends up with us doing things we don't want to do and not feeling good about it in the process, like agreeing to go to a friend's party, even though every bone in our body is crying out for a relaxing bath and an early night.

Do you find it hard to say "no" to people? It's an ongoing challenge for me, and it still feels very awkward sometimes.

Knowing our energetic limits and sticking to them presents a fabulous opportunity for looking after ourselves in ways that often require saying "no." I used to automatically say "yes" whenever a friend asked to meet up. Even if I already had a busy week and felt stressed, I'd still find a way to squeeze them in. I also used to say "yes" to people whose company I found energetically draining, which never felt good.

Taking on too much is depleting; it comes at a great personal cost, and it can take a while to restore your energy and achieve a higher vibration. So, I decided to make some changes by spring-cleaning my boundaries. These days, I conserve my energy by ensuring I have plenty of rejuvenating activities in my week and making wise decisions regarding time spent socializing. When my plate feels full, I say "no" to myself or others. Maintaining a healthy balance is my priority. And I'm much more discerning about who I see, focusing on those who nourish my soul.

Self-prioritization may sound like a distant dream to you, especially if you're looking after babies, young children, ill or elderly friends, or relatives. Some people who we care for genuinely need a great deal of assistance. In these circumstances, it can be challenging to make time for ourselves, whether going to the gym, a yoga class, meeting a friend for tea, visiting the dentist, or having a weekend off. Your needs must be met too. Maybe you can find trustworthy home help with your youngsters or sign them up for a wonderful daycare facility. When my kids were small, they attended day care a couple of afternoons a week. During my time off, I exercised and got a few jobs done. It made a world of difference, giving me a much-needed break, particularly because James was unable to share the childcare duties as he worked long hours and had a lengthy commute.

If you're caring for people who are unwell or elderly, be open to finding creative solutions to give you some time for yourself. Use respite care or home assistance or ask friends or family members to help out so you can have valuable time away to take good care of your own needs. The truth is, we're not much good to others when we're not looking after ourselves very well, and we can quickly feel burned out, depleted, and resentful. So, taking necessary breaks, a way of saying "yes" to ourselves, is very important. Not only do we benefit from nourishing our mind, body, and spirit, but so do the people we care for. Everyone benefits.

Easily overlooked but just as important is the ability to say "no" to our powerful, unwanted behavior patterns when they rear up. It might be an irresistible urge to criticize ourselves or others, engage in people pleasing, check the news online for the umpteenth time, spend hours on social media, eat an entire tub of chocolate ice cream, or buy stuff we don't need or can't afford. We all have patterns of some kind. There is no judgment here!

Despite believing we're powerless to their allure, we're not. We have the choice to refuse to run the behavior pattern. Admittedly, stopping these automatic programs can require tremendous strength and willpower. But we have the power to do it. When we refuse to play along in the old ways, over time, it weakens those ingrained patterns. When we feel the urge to do something that we know isn't good for us, instead of automatically going ahead, it's helpful to pause and breathe deeply for a few minutes. Refuse to budge. Go for a walk, take a shower or bath, dance, meditate, or do something else that appeals to switch up the pattern. Keep breathing through the discomfort, however strong it blows. Be still, and I guarantee the intensity will fade.

Speaking of pausing: In my experience, one of the best things we can do for ourselves when someone requests a response from us is to take a moment before replying. Waiting is a fabulous pattern interrupt and gives us space to check in with ourselves for our true, heartfelt answer, instead of giving a hurried, knee-jerk reaction. Pausing facilitates a loosening of the people-pleasing pattern and gives us a break from feeling under pressure to give a rapid response.

Perhaps the prevalence of emails, phone calls, texting, and the multitude of messaging apps available to us contributes to our sense of urgency to immediately reply. The chances are, in most circumstances, the other person can wait until you're ready to respond. It's safe to say, "Let me think about that; I'll get back to you," or "I'm not sure; let me sit with it for a while." It's perfectly fine to take a day or more before you send that text or have that conversation.

Pausing gives you the opportunity to discover how you truly feel about whatever is being asked of you. Your body is a fabulous tool for discerning what is a good fit for you. The body never lies; it's a reliable truth-teller. All that's required of us is to tune into our body and become aware of its response.

How do you answer from your body rather than from your mind? Try this. Imagine yourself doing the very thing you've been asked to do. It's essential to act as if it's happening right now, looking through your own eyes, seeing what you see, hearing what you hear, feeling what you feel, and noticing any self-talk. Then, scan your body to notice the physical sensations you're experiencing. If it feels expansive, light, loving, positive, or warm, it's probably a "yes;" if it feels tight, painful, blocked, or constricted, it's likely a "no."

It can be hard to determine our body's response in the presence of others because we may be feeling under pressure, distracted, tense, or stuck in our thoughts. So, until we become well practiced at deciphering its messages, it's a good idea to nip out to a private, quiet space, like the bathroom, or pop outside so you can fully focus on what your body is telling you about the situation. If you're unclear or feeling blocked, perhaps sitting with it in meditation or asking for your body's response when you feel very relaxed will be helpful. Play around with it, and above all else, trust what your body tells you.

I used to over-explain my "no" responses. It was an extremely disempowering habit that diminished my light. My justification often felt like a runaway train, and the more I spoke, the worse I felt. I now realize that was my people-pleasing pattern at play, trying to make them feel better about my "no," believing it would all be okay if they understood my reasons. It felt so much lighter when I stopped that bad habit and instead kept my responses kind, firm, and concise. Honestly, I think everyone was relieved when I packed that in!

Creating healthy boundaries and strengthening our self-love muscles also involves making necessary changes when situations or relationships are detrimental to us. In extreme cases, that may mean we must distance ourselves from family members, end a romantic relationship or friendship, or leave a business partnership. We may sense it's time to begin standing up for ourselves — to express how we feel, say "no" when we need to, or ask without expectation for our needs to be met. Perhaps, sometimes, it's a wake-up call to break our people-pleasing patterns and prioritize our own needs.

The complex and troublesome relationship with my dad was a perfect example of how I needed to create and enforce healthy boundaries. After each upsetting episode with him, I brushed his behavior aside and optimistically believed it would be better next time. I hoped that he would mellow with age and that we would reach a point where we would get along and enjoy each other's company without triggering each other.

My last-ever trip to see my dad in Cornwall was outrageously stressful because his behavior was extremely unpleasant. He was angry, argumentative, and verbally aggressive towards me. I repeatedly tried to steer our conversations into happier waters but failed miserably.

I'd had enough of his mistreatment, so I stood up to him and deflected his attacks. I refused to be his victim any longer. My response to his behavior didn't sit well with him; it actually made him worse. He wasn't used to people calling out his bad behavior.

Although I did my best to stay calm, I got triggered by his behavior. It was an extremely upsetting and exhausting few days.

On my drive back to Heathrow Airport, I made a monumental decision and declared that I would never again visit him in Cornwall. It was too damaging for me, and the personal cost was too high.

I admitted to myself that my dad was incapable of having healthy, close relationships. He wasn't the kind of person you could have deep and meaningful conversations with about anything. So, I knew it was pointless trying to explore if we could heal our relationship.

Over the next five months, we were in radio silence. I needed a lot of space from him. My creative buzz vanished into thin air, and I didn't paint for months afterward. With my head spinning from our encounter, I needed time to recover and heal my wounds.

I came to a place of peace with the stark possibility that he might die before I was ready to speak with him or see him again. I wasn't being dramatic about that either. Having had previous major heart surgery, two strokes during the COVID lockdown, and being eighty-two years old, he was on borrowed time.

It was an extremely tough decision, and it brought up a lot of guilt, sadness, and hurt in me. However, I chose to be true to myself, put my needs first, and stand in my power. I was never going to give him the chance to behave like that towards me again.

Although it doesn't always feel good to enforce healthy boundaries, it's crucial to listen to our inner voice, be brave, and stand up for ourselves.

Another common problem for those of us with boundary issues is struggling to ask for help. We may desperately want to delegate to lessen our load but find it difficult to speak up. This has shown up for me mainly concerning domestic chores.

As a child, I was expected to perform domestic duties because my mum was absent, and I was the only female in the household. I felt resentful about it at the time, which, years later, made it hard for me to ask my kids to help at home. I would ask them to do things, and they would magically disappear or come up with creative reasons why they couldn't do it, or they'd just flat out refuse. I backed down, not wanting to force them. I felt angry and disrespected but couldn't bring myself to talk to my kids about it.

As an empty nester, I've taken positive steps to rectify this. Although asking for their assistance still feels uncomfortable, I do it, and they step up. Firming up my boundaries with them and asking for their help have created an even deeper bond between us, and I feel more respected and valued. I love the energy that fills our home when we all contribute to household tasks.

As a sensitive empath, I tend to take on the energy of others: family, friends, clients, people I come across in passing, and the collective. I find myself experiencing strong, heavy emotions without always knowing their source. Carrying these energies from others can weigh us down and undermine our well-being.

Here's a quick and easy technique to clear out those energies:

- Take some deep breaths, in through your nose and out through your mouth, breathing in spaciousness and breathing out tension.

- After a few minutes, when you're feeling relaxed, invite your soul fully into your physical body through your crown chakra. Sense the energy of your soul moving down through you and filling you up, all the way to your fingers, toes, and eyelashes.

- Then imagine an energetic cord emanating from your root chakra at the base of your spine and connecting with the core of Mother Earth. Take a moment to feel the beneficial effects of our planet's grounding energy as it migrates up into your body and energy field. Sense your powerful and healing connection to this grounding force. Take some deep breaths.

♦ Then, gently bring your awareness to your heart space, and from a place of stillness, invite *Divine Love* to enter your crown chakra and fill up your physical body — drenching your cells and the spaces in between, before saturating your energy field.

♦ With your body and aura filled up with the energy of your soul, Mother Earth, and *Divine Love*, the energy of other people is effortlessly displaced.

♦ Be present with this experience for a while. Let the energy you have taken on from others continue to be released. As it vacates, the spaces left behind are automatically filled by the energy of *Love*.

♦ Perhaps you can notice how clear you feel now — so much lighter than before. Before coming back to full waking consciousness, say thank you to your deeper self for this shift.

♦ I recommend using this tool to clear yourself out whenever you sense you've taken on the energy of others. You can incorporate it as part of your toolbox for daily energetic hygiene and use it as often as you like. Some people love to do it a few times each day. Play around with it, tweak it, and find out what works best for you.

If you're highly intuitive, you may sense the thoughts, feelings, beliefs, and patterns of others, picking up on all their stuff. I used to feel bombarded by all the information coming my way, so I created clear boundaries for myself by turning off my intuitive abilities when needed. I imagine it like a light switch and just flick it off. As far as I'm concerned, it's none of my business what's going on with anyone else unless I'm being asked to assist them.

When we clean up our boundaries, we may encounter a variety of responses from others. They may applaud us and support our positive shift, or they may push against us. They may be used to us showing up in a particular way; perhaps they benefited from our people-pleasing behavior. It can be hard to accept that their reaction isn't personal, but it really isn't. Most people focus on getting their own needs met and aren't terribly keen on change. They may refuse to accept our new behavior, or try to demean, silence, or argue with us. They might blame and attack rather than be supportive. Be prepared for all or any of the above.

It's helpful to devise a plan to deal with negative reactions. We can ignore their response and maintain our position without giving in or needing to justify our actions. Or maybe it feels aligned to have an honest conversation with them about what isn't working for us and sharing that we need to look after ourselves better by making some changes. If their negative response continues, we may need to keep enforcing our boundaries until they realize we mean it. In some cases, we might decide to distance ourselves from them for a while, or in extreme cases, we might even decide to end the relationship. The bottom line is that we get to choose who we have in our lives.

It's best to start practicing new healthy boundaries on relatively insignificant things. Regular practice on the smaller stuff allows us to gradually become more comfortable and confident in speaking up about what we want and need. We strengthen our boundary muscles. Then, when more difficult situations arise, it's much easier to enforce our boundaries, deepening our capacity to love ourselves and improving our relationships with others.

Setting boundaries is a powerful way of looking after ourselves with love and respect. During meditation or quiet time, you have a wonderful opportunity to tap into your inner guidance and ask what the best boundaries are for yourself in any given situation. Only you know what they are; listen to your own wisdom rather than automatically taking on what others suggest. Trust yourself.

Please do your best to be compassionate and gentle with yourself as you navigate these waters of boundary issues. It can be challenging. Rather than being hard on yourself if you find yourself back in people-pleasing territory, I lovingly urge you to focus on celebrating the times when you do a great job of taking care of your own needs first. Let go of needing to get it right all the time; messing up is fine. The important thing is to keep practicing.

You've got this. I believe in you.

# 7

# GIFTS FROM ADVERSITY

At the heart of this chapter lies the realization that gems come out of even difficult and traumatic situations and events. Instead of repeatedly focusing on the same old stories from our pasts about what happened and who did what to whom, we can notice the gifts that arose from our pain and trauma. Without fail, however big or small, these gifts are always there. Be patient, though, as it can take a while for us to notice them. The more we can open to this concept, the faster the gems reveal themselves, and the quicker we can incorporate the realizations and heal ourselves from the past.

The idea that there can be gems in difficult situations might be new to you, and you might find it incomprehensible or impossible to believe. If that's the case, that's okay — just stay with me on this.

Take a moment to bring to your mind a challenging event you experienced. It's best to begin with one that isn't too extreme. Ask yourself what good things came from that experience. There may be initial resistance from the mind, but no worries. Let yourself know that all resistance is welcome and embrace it. Notice how it is simply a protective aspect of yourself. Stay open and be curious. Answers may come immediately, or they may show up in your mind at some future point. Let the gems come to you rather than desperately trying to identify them. When they arrive, express your gratitude to the Universe for the gift and fully receive it deep inside.

When painful old stories re-emerge, instead of paying attention to them and letting them derail you again, do your best to focus on the positive things that arose from them. Over time, intentionally re-directing your focus through the repeated action of "not that, but this" weakens the power of the old experiences and creates new desirable neural pathways in your brain.

Focusing on the aspects that benefited us helps us escape the powerful, tenacious clutches of well-worn ruts of suffering.

I've done this so much that I genuinely feel grateful for my troubled childhood. After a while, the gifts began to outweigh the pain.

To illustrate this concept, I'm diving into the topic of parenting, which includes being parented, along with being a parent when you've had a crap upbringing, and lastly, on becoming a loving parent for our inner children.

In each section, I mention a handful of challenges from my life before flipping into some of the key gifts I've received because of them. Notice what is evoked in you as you read them; if it resonates, take some time to reflect on your experiences.

*Note: Even if you're not a parent, you may find valuable insights in this section that contribute to your transformation.*

Let's dive in!

I've selected a few notable things to share about being parented.

One day when I was around nine, my brother and I were sitting at the breakfast table with our parents. We'd recently relocated from Harrogate, North Yorkshire, to Croesyceiliog, South Wales. It was an unsettling, and difficult time for all of us. The horrendous arguments between my parents continued, casting a miserable, shameful shadow over our home.

That day, Dad asked John and me if Mum should leave. I looked at my brother, who is two years my senior, desperately wanting him to speak up for both of us. He remained silent. A part of me knew that something had to change. We couldn't go on living in that toxic environment. So, I blurted out, "I think she should go."

Courageously speaking up that day had massive ramifications for our family. My mum moved back to Yorkshire to live with her boyfriend, and our home life was turned upside down. We only saw her a few times each year after that. It felt like she'd left my life. We lived with Dad, who neglected us both and scared me.

I carried the painful burden of speaking up that day for many decades. I felt guilty even though I knew that I should never have been put in that no-win situation by my parents' irresponsible behavior. Unsurprisingly, it created a deeply ingrained pattern in me: avoiding speaking up in tough situations.

My parents both had unhealthy responses to problems. At the first sign of trouble, they immediately switched into disaster mode. Even the smallest of problems or inconveniences were treated as a nightmare. They snapped into an intensely stressed, anxious, fearful, and self-critical state.

As I shared with you in Chapter 3, as young children, we automatically soak in the thoughts, beliefs, and behaviors of those around us. They become part of our belief systems and automatic responses and behaviors, even if they are extreme or unhealthy.

My nervous system became hardwired to adopt this bizarre behavior as normal and acceptable. It was a crazy way to exist. I lived my life in a fearful state, wary of potential problems, and expecting everything to go wrong. I didn't question it for many years. It's taken a lot of love and attention to weaken this damaging and unhealthy conditioned response in me. When life gets seriously rough, it can still flare up sometimes.

Growing up without my mum in my daily life and living with a stressed, volatile, and negligent father was challenging and painful. I felt abandoned, rejected, unworthy, and unlovable.

When I was a teenager, my dad told me I would never amount to anything worthwhile. He told me not to bother applying to university because I wouldn't get in and would end up working at the grocery store check-out. I was bombarded by criticism and given no guidance or support from him.

It was a tough upbringing, but my experiences produced an abundance of valuable gifts. They revealed themselves to me after I began healing my emotional wounds. In doing so, I moved out of a place of victimhood and into one of freedom.

For a start, I was determined to prove my dad wrong about me. I strove to show him that I was intelligent and valuable and would make a great life for myself. That belligerent energy helped me to create space from my childhood and was the powerful force behind setting a new and improved direction in my life. It drove me to leave Winchester, an unhealthy place for me, and go to Sheffield University. It was the key driving force behind achieving impressive grades in my undergraduate degree, and it was still running when I excelled in my master's degree.

A few years later, I realized that the pattern of proving him wrong had run out of steam. I saw how exhausting it had been; yet, I could also see that it had improved my life. It was a massive relief when I realized I didn't need to prove him wrong anymore. I was free of my old life, and I was self-sufficient. From that moment onwards, I chose to do things that were based on moving towards what I wanted rather than moving away from his mistreatment of me.

As my healing journey continued, I began appreciating that I'm a survivor through and through — an independent, resilient, and determined soul. My deep compassion and lack of judgment stem from having seen and experienced a lot of darkness in my life. We're all doing our best, with a positive intent for ourselves, even if that causes problems for others.

My intense pain propelled me onto my spiritual journey of awakening. On that path, I've met some truly incredible, inspiring human beings who have touched my life in magnificent and powerful ways. I wouldn't change that for anything.

Through healing sessions, becoming certified in various healing modalities, and immersing myself in Gangaji's teachings, I've transformed my life in the most beautiful ways.

With a tremendous sense of freedom from my emotional wounds and an open, compassionate heart, I began attracting clients seeking support and guidance.

It's truly an honor to partner with people who have experienced painful pasts and want to free themselves from their suffering.

The energetic imprints from my childhood, combined with over eighteen years on my healing journey, empower me to guide others on their healing paths. These experiences have given me the wisdom, humility, and resonance to partner with clients in loving and powerful ways.

I firmly believe that we are all capable of healing ourselves and improving our lives by leaving the past behind. If I can do it, so can you.

Without the pain and suffering that emanated from my upbringing, I wouldn't have had a deep desire to serve others. I'm grateful that so many people have improved their lives because of what happened to me.

Thankfully, I've shifted from disaster thinking to responding to problems in life in calmer and more resourceful ways. It does resurface now and then, but I usually snap out of it quickly and know how to rebound energetically.

For many years, I was fixated on what I perceived to be the negative parts of my parents' personalities. However, as I continued to heal from my wounds, I began to see the totality of them.

With Dad, I'd overlooked that he was a talented musician with a great sense of humor at times. He loved learning and spoke four languages, earning a Ph.D. in Maritime History when he was seventy. He continued cycling into his eighties. His bike only gathered dust when the UK government banned cycling during the COVID lockdown. And after two strokes, he tenaciously fought his way back to regaining his fitness, balance, and speech.

So, the whole picture is that he was a mixture of great things and challenging parts. I've come to understand that I needed far more from him as a father than he could offer me. For whatever reason, he just wasn't wired that way. After Mum left, he could have deserted us, too, but he didn't. He stayed.

With my mum, I came to appreciate, with deep compassion, that she did her best at the time. Quite simply, she needed to get out of her terrible marriage. Her desire to be happy led her into a relationship with someone who gave her the love and attention that she desired and deserved.

She honestly believed that we'd have a better life being brought up by a university-educated dad than by her.

My mum has plenty of wonderful attributes, including fierce loyalty to those she loves and being made of extraordinarily strong stuff. Although I find this frustrating at times, she's probably the most determined person I know, and that's served her well with her health challenges. She's also blessed with a brilliant sense of humor and is talented in the musical department.

After graduation, when my money was extremely tight, she was always happy to help me out financially when I most needed it.

As a grandmother, she was very helpful and supportive with my kids when they were little. She was always delighted to visit from afar and throw herself into the mix of playing with and caring for them.

Not only did I come to see my parents in their fullness, but I was also able to forgive them for everything that had happened. It didn't necessarily mean I wanted to be extremely close to them, but it improved our relationship.

After all, we're only human, and none of us are perfect. We are all flawed to some degree. Having high expectations about anyone, including ourselves, is unrealistic and unhealthy.

Lastly, I'm eternally grateful for how I was brought up because it set the tone for how I showed up as a parent. I knew what it felt like to grow up feeling unloved, neglected, and unsupported, and I wanted something so much better for my kids. I was determined to be there for them in every way I could. I wanted them to know in every cell of their bodies that they were loved unconditionally and that I supported, respected, and valued them.

I became a mother at the age of twenty-seven. The early years of motherhood were a highly demanding time for me. Partly because I didn't have a clue how to deal with babies and children, it was a scary and daunting adjustment to become responsible for another life, and I went through agonizing hell with breastfeeding problems. My daughter, Jess, was an unsettled, colicky baby who didn't sleep well at night. James was working long hours, often sleeping at the office and working straight through weekends. He wasn't around much to give me a break. With minimal support, I felt alone. I had to dig deep to get through it.

Although I adored my gorgeous baby girl, I was tired, miserable, and overwhelmed. I recall having these thoughts: *I've got to get this right; I have to do this all by myself; I'm a terrible mother;* and in the most harrowing moments, thinking, *Oh my God, what have I done?!*

Thankfully, at that challenging time, I was blessed to have a caring and extremely humorous friend, Annabelle, in my life. We'd met in National Childbirth Trust classes and formed a firm friendship. Both of our babies were a bit of a handful with similar issues. Annabelle got me through those outrageously difficult months. We met regularly, drank gallons of tea, and ate a lot of toast with hummus as we shared about our lives and the babies. We laughed long and hard. The Universe had sent an angel my way; she was a lifesaver. I dread to think how I would have coped without her help, generosity, and humor.

My son was born a couple of years later. Life became even more of a juggling act, and at the same time, I adored being a mother of two.

Despite my fierce and deep love for them both, as time passed by, disturbing thoughts began to surface in my mind, especially when I was stressed and overwhelmed by parenting. A part of me wanted to escape, to have space for myself. I was worried that it might be in my genes to leave my kids when the going got tough, as my mum had done. It was always there, a nagging fear in the back of my mind.

Raising Jess was particularly eventful at times. There was never a dull moment. When she was about six, her room often looked like a bomb had hit it. Toys, tiaras, magic wands, and princess outfits were strewn all over the carpet. When asked to tidy up, she refused to do so. I'd had enough; so, one day, getting very frustrated and upset, I insisted that if she didn't tidy up, I would put everything in a black bin bag and throw it out. Defiant, she didn't budge. While she was at school, I put her toys into a rubbish bag and stowed it safely in a storage cupboard in the attic. When Jess returned home, she was furious. In retaliation, she fetched a black rubbish bag and emptied my drawers, shoving my clothes into the bag!

Like most parents, I was sometimes bereft of ideas on

what to do for the best. When my son was very young, he would sulk for days, hiding behind curtains and refusing to speak to me if he didn't get his way. My attempts to coax him out of his funk failed miserably; he stubbornly held his ground. It was very upsetting for me when he distanced himself. I felt I was doing a terrible job and was completely stumped.

All in all, I found it extremely tough being a parent. I struggled when I didn't know the best approach to take when challenges arose. Jess and Josh were experts at pushing my buttons, sometimes triggering them all simultaneously! Back then, winding me up seemed to be an entertaining pastime for them.

To be perfectly honest, the teenage years almost broke me. It was horrendous at times. I'm not providing details here because that's our private family life, but suffice it to say that we had to deal with some challenging situations.

I used to compare myself to other parents, and in my mind, I always came up short, which resulted in tremendous pain and self-judgment. I felt inadequate and unprepared for the role of mother. Others seemed to be natural parents who demonstrated clear, healthy boundaries with ease and knew how to respond in level-headed, resourceful ways to issues that arose. It felt awful when I believed my negative thoughts about my parenting skills, and I blamed my perceived inadequacies on the lack of great parental role models in my childhood.

Enforcing boundaries was particularly tricky for me. As I discussed in an earlier chapter, this has been an ongoing challenge in my life. My permeable boundaries showed up a lot in parenting. When I asked my kids to do chores around the home, they smelled my weakness, like horses sensing fear. I received imaginative excuses about why they couldn't do them or they magically vanished into thin air when I needed them. It was an exhausting cycle that required immense energy to get them to follow through.

From the age of twelve, I'd been expected to wash clothes, iron my dad's shirts, and cook meals for my dad and brother. I'd resented the role I was forced to play as a teenager. I caved in so easily with Jess and Josh because I didn't want them to carry a heavy domestic burden as I'd had to.

As a mother, there were times when I felt undervalued, disrespected, taken advantage of, resentful, and disappointed. I was tired of carrying so much of the domestic load. I now see that my kids' behavior was triggering an old pattern from my childhood. A younger part of me was still hurting and angry about what had happened to her.

Okay, moving on to the gifts.

As I parented Jess and Josh, loving them and looking after them, I created the kind of upbringing that I would have loved for myself. I had so much fun with my kids and delighted in spending time with them! As I did so, my heart and inner child healed, little by little. It was a priceless gift, for sure.

Our lives were full, with plenty of love, cuddles, reading stories, chatting with them, taking them to Tumble Tots, ballet, swimming, football, tennis, Brownies and Boy Scouts, and whatever else they were up to. Together, we spent countless hours playing games together and baking tasty treats. We always had creative projects underway, often involving lots of glitter and glue!

In those years when the kids were home, my heart opened, and I learned how to love unconditionally. I adored them both and realized that there was no way I could ever leave them.

As I lightened the load from my own childhood wounds, self-compassion appeared. And I forgave myself for finding parenting tough. I accepted my mothering skills with all my imperfections. I loved my kids beyond words; I was there for them. I acknowledged that in the absence of good role models, I was doing a great job, always digging deep to parent to the best of my ability. I realized how proud of myself I was and still am. Despite the rocky road I've traveled, I managed to dance through motherhood, the highs and the lows, in loving, caring, and fulfilling ways. Being a mother has been and continues to be an enormous blessing in my life and an essential part of my healing journey.

In addition to forgiving myself, I forgave Jess and Josh for giving me a hard time over the years. I realized it's just what kids do, pushing their parents to the edge sometimes, especially those youngsters with a lot of creativity, intelligence, complexity, and determination.

The gift of accepting people and events as they are, rather than wishing they were different somehow, has been a tremendously valuable gem acquired from my spiritual journey. I've learned to accept my daughter and son for who they are, and I let go of believing any thoughts that they needed to change. I saw the arrogance in my behavior and noticed my fierce control mechanisms at work when I tried to manage them. They are incredible human beings, exactly as they are — genuinely wonderful, characterful, willful, loving human beings.

When I improved my boundaries, they responded well. These days, when they visit, they contribute to the smooth running of the household, and I feel respected and valued by them.

Throughout his eighty-two years, my dad never apologized to me for his behavior. That didn't feel good. So, when I became a parent, I decided to make sure that I apologized to my kids when I behaved in ways that were out of order. I used to have a bad temper and was well-known for being argumentative. If I'd come on a bit strong, I'd take some quiet time to reflect on what had happened. Once I'd calmed down and gained clarity, I'd have an honest conversation with them, telling them that I loved them, apologizing for losing my temper, and explaining why I reacted the way I did.

My dad's parenting skills ended up being a driving force in making me a better parent.

As my children grew up, I led with love as much as possible. I focused on values of respect, honesty, and good communication, doing my best to take care of them from a place of humility and personal responsibility.

I miss them living with me. I doubt I'll ever get used to it. However, I'm so proud of who they have become as adults. They are both loving, free thinkers, independent, capable, and resourceful in different ways. I'm proud that I brought them up in a way that bolstered their belief that they could manage by themselves during the COVID pandemic.

They continue to be cornerstones in my existence through their ongoing support and encouragement. Even though they reckon that some of my ideas are unconventional and my eccentric nature amuses them no end, they accept me for who I am. What a lucky person I am to have their presence in my life.

Lastly, let's move on to nurturing our relationship with our inner children, which is a powerful ally in healing from our past hurts.

For those of you unfamiliar with this concept of our inner children, I encourage you to keep an open mind and heart as you read this. Give yourself permission to experience this kind of loving and nourishing relationship.

Younger versions of ourselves exist inside our psyche. Even though we can't touch them with our physical hands, and most of us are unable to see them with our eyes, they are there, and we can connect with them. They often show up when clients work with me, and they are regular visitors in my own life.

Sometimes, when we look within, we become aware of a particular inner child — us at a specific age when something significant occurred — calling for our love and attention. At other times, more than one inner child may appear — ranging from a couple to a large gathering of inner children.

Communicating with our inner children and parenting them in healthy and loving ways can genuinely transform our lives for the better.

This practice centers around developing a supportive parental relationship with our younger selves, imbued with love, trust, respect, and compassion. When we give voice to our younger selves and listen to them, accepting every single aspect of who they are — regardless of how angry, scared, resistant, or hostile they may seem — and let them know that we're there for them no matter what, it changes our lives. They relax, soften, and blossom when they hear our adult selves reassuring them: *I love you. I've got you! I'll always be here to look after you.*

I believe that they appear in our mind's eye when we have some unresolved emotional baggage from a particular time in our lives that is still energetically active inside of us, driving our behavior from behind the scenes, and is ready for healing and release. These aspects of us may be traumatized, very fearful, and too scared to let us move forward. Their behavior can prevent us from experiencing the best possible health, wonderful relationships, and fulfilling careers we desire. Our wounded inner children can be the invisible reason we struggle in life. By communicating with them in a loving, caring way, listening to their needs, and providing them with the attention, encouragement, and support they ask for, the inner conflict vanishes, leaving us free to step forward in a new, improved way.

Here's a personal example. I've never been one to harp on about how much better and easier my life would have been if only I'd had a great childhood with loving parents who supported and nurtured me. I didn't think living in a fantasy world would be beneficial. Even though I was struggling, I always made the best of the situation, tried to stay positive and resourceful, and kept moving forward.

During an EMDR session with a therapist, a younger me, about five years old, came to light in my mind's eye. She was screaming with ferocious intensity, *It's not fair!* From her perspective, she was angry about her family dynamics, how she had been treated, and the problems it had created in her life. To her, it was unjust. In that session, she let the adult me know her feelings: *Others have it so much better than I do! I missed out on so much! I wish I had a close family like they do. It's not fair!*

In an instant, I saw how I hadn't acknowledged the part of me that believed she'd been dealt a crappy hand and that life had been profoundly unfair. I'd spent decades dismissing that younger me, and in doing so, I'd avoided experiencing her self-pity, regret, shame, and sadness. I'd ignored how she felt, stuffing her emotions and beliefs deep inside of me in tightly secured boxes as I tried to be a successful and functioning human being. She was ready to make her presence known to me. She was showing up to express how she felt and wanted to feel better.

I'd never had much time for those who claimed life was unfair. I'd regarded feeling sorry for oneself as a weakness and a terrible strategy for surviving and thriving. In my eyes, you had to be strong and not let life get you down.

That day in my therapist's office, when this younger me showed up with her *It's not fair!* energy and shared how she felt, my response was to give her all the energetic space and permission she needed to release those intense emotions. A massive outpouring of anguish and hurt occurred. I let her roar and rage without judgment. It felt like a ball of energy, tangled into endless tight knots in my throat, was finally unraveling with ease. Tears poured down my cheeks.

Throughout it all, in my mind's eye, I held her in a loving embrace and told her I fully accepted the totality of her feelings and beliefs. As the energy was discharged and she calmed down, I soothed, reassured, and mothered her, letting her know I'd always be here for her. In a nutshell, I gave her what I'd most needed as a youngster.

As the sadness, anger, and resentment dissipated, I found myself in a calm place, feeling unconditional love and acceptance for myself and events in my life. A tremendous sense of relief arose.

It requires a lot of energy to keep our intense emotions under lock and key. When we release them, we experience a genuine sense of liberation, freeing up energy for other endeavors.

A flash of valuable insight showed me that I was triggered by others when they claimed that life wasn't fair because there was a younger aspect of Rachel, who I'd been unaware of, who truly felt that way. The other people were merely a mirror of what was alive and kicking inside me that I had been rejecting.

Thankfully, a tender, loving, and gentle healing occurred during my EMDR sessions. It felt amazing to connect with the younger aspects of myself and give them the comfort, reassurance of safety, and love that they desperately needed.

As I deepened my loving relationship with my inner children, my guides shared some fabulous tools with me to encourage and boost the healing process. I use them with my inner youngsters and those of my clients. If they appeal to you, give them a go. Adopting them will enhance your life and increase your capacity to love yourself.

If you're new to connecting with your inner children, at first, it's often easiest to sense your inner child when you're sitting quietly and are free from interruptions and distractions. As you develop your relationships with them, you will likely find that you can communicate with them wherever you are, regardless of what is happening around you.

### GROUP HUG

I particularly love this one for when we wake up in the morning. Instead of mulling over your to-do list or thinking about problems, have a group hug instead. It feels sublime. Simply invite your younger selves for a tender, loving embrace. They get to choose if they participate or not. Either way, it's fine. It's a brilliant way of checking in with your collective of younger selves to see how they are doing. If you discover anyone is out of sorts, you can give them a voice to express anything they need to share with you. They may have some guidance for you. Listen to them, support and encourage them. Let them know that they are safe and loved by you.

Perhaps you'll sense how delighted they are to be included and how harmonious it feels for them to begin their day in this gentle way.

## IN THE THICK OF IT

Another practice is to connect with your inner children when life is rough. If we've been triggered by someone or an event and find ourselves deep in dense emotions like anger, fear, sadness, guilt, or hurt, it's very helpful to take our awareness inside to find out what's going on in our inner community. We often discover one or more younger parts struggling and longing for love and support.

Be a loving parent towards them. Ask how you can support them. Perhaps they need to vent. Are they scared of something? Are they trying to stop you from taking a particular action, or are they letting you know they mistrust a particular person? What would they like you to do or stop doing? Be gentle with them and listen deeply.

If you had childhood difficulties with your dad or other men, connecting with your Divine masculine energy and directing it to your inner child might be beneficial. If "mother wounding" was part of your upbringing, then directing Divine feminine energies to younger parts might be healing.

Formative years involving issues with both parents, as mine were, may call for loving, supportive energies from both the Divine masculine and feminine.

There is no formula here. Simply ask your inner child what would help them and what they need. Going with the flow is always the best approach that leads to the best possible outcome.

## CIRCLE OF LOVE

During a meditation at my NLP Master Practitioner's Training Course, I had a profoundly transformative experience. A circle of Rachels, sitting on the ground, appeared in my mind's eye. Every age of my life was represented, from birth to death.

I was shown a practice of inviting any Rachels who were struggling in some way into the center of the circle. From there, they looked out to see the remaining Rachels beaming *Love* towards them, giving them all the support, acceptance, compassion, and healing that they required.

When I'm in the center of the circle, a protective, warm glow of energy fills my entire being. It feels ecstatic, and I sense I'm being seen, heard, and met on every level. Dense emotions dissipate, and I feel noticeably lighter.

Play with this tool and create a supportive, healing, loving inner collective for yourself, comprised of you through all the ages. This powerful, nurturing circle is always available to you, wherever you are and at any time of day.

I encourage you to notice the gifts that have arisen from whatever has happened in your life. Focus on them and how they have enhanced your life rather than on the old stories.

Above all else, be gentle with yourself, celebrate those gems, and if it's available to you right now, lean into forgiving everyone, including yourself.

# PART 2

# Awakening

# 8

# A BREATH OF FRESH AIR

Most of us take our breathing for granted and rarely give it much attention. It happens automatically, all by itself, without us needing to think about doing it. Play along with me. As you read this, bring your awareness to your breath, without changing it, and just notice how you're breathing. Are you taking shallow sips of air, or are you taking relaxed deep breaths? As I write this, my breathing is very shallow, with air barely reaching beyond my throat. My ribs are hardly moving.

By observing our breathing at different times, we discover our habitual patterns. When feeling stressed, anxious, or overwhelmed, many of us take rapid, short breaths with minimal oxygen intake. If we do this a lot, over time, shallow breathing can become detrimental to the healthy functioning of our bodies, mainly because we're not getting enough oxygen. The good news is that there are easy breathing techniques we can adopt to boost our overall well-being.

Some breathing techniques are extraordinarily effective at activating our relaxation response, calming our nervous system, and helping our bodies rebalance and heal themselves. In addition to reducing stress levels and anxiety, conscious breathing is a great way to escape our thoughts and connect with our bodies, effortlessly bringing us into the present moment. This practice clears our minds of clutter and negative thoughts and helps us to focus, improving clarity on circumstances in our lives. Managing our breathing is a wonderful and powerful self-love tool that's always available to us and costs nothing to implement.

For many decades, I was oblivious to my breathing habits. Sure, during exercise I used specific breathing techniques as instructed by yoga and Pilates teachers, and I diligently followed the midwives' breathing protocols during childbirth. But I was largely unaware of my breathing the rest of the time.

When I tuned into my breathing, I discovered that I take in around 10 percent of a full breath when I'm uptight or overwhelmed. I do the same when concentrating on a task, like writing. Miniscule amounts of air manage to enter my lungs. What's your default mode of breathing? I invite you to observe how you breathe through your daily life. Check in during challenging moments, when you're focusing on a task, being creative, driving, at work, at health appointments, watching TV, and in the company of others. Become familiar with your own patterns. With awareness of how you're breathing, you can begin to make deliberate changes to support your emotional, physical, and mental health.

Let me take you on a short journey inside to boost your sense of well-being. Begin by taking some bigger inhalations, but be gentle; don't force this. Draw air deep into your lungs and belly and breathe out fully — filling the front, sides, and back of your ribcage. Think of your ribs as a big cylinder that moves in every direction, to the front, sides, and back, expanding your chest cavity in all planes.

A great way to develop familiarity with full ribcage breathing is to place your hands lightly on your ribcage and feel the movements of your chest cavity as you breathe. Please know that breathing into the back of the ribcage is often the most challenging for individuals, as we rarely devote much attention to the back of our bodies. If that is the case for you, this might help: bring additional awareness to the back of your ribs by placing your hands there. Visualize breathing into the area under your hands and feel them rising and falling until it becomes more natural.

Once full ribcage breathing is established, do your best to keep your shoulders relaxed. There's no need for your shoulders to rise to your ears as you breathe in. Bring air into your body by letting your ribcage expand instead of moving your shoulders up and down. Practice breathing without your shoulders getting involved and focus on expanding and contracting your ribcage. Relax your shoulders and let them rest. And be patient, as it can be a deeply ingrained pattern that might take a little practice to shift.

Let's develop this a little further. As you continue taking long, deep breaths into all of your ribcage, with relaxed shoulders, let go of any tension in your belly. Then, focus on guiding your inhalation down the central channel of your body that runs from your crown chakra to your root chakra. Imagine this channel as a golden pillar of light. Visualize or feel your breath entering your body through your crown chakra, traveling down your golden central channel, bringing energy to each chakra one at a time and lighting them up sequentially, like stops on a pinball machine. Visualize infusing your crown chakra, your third eye, onto your throat chakra, flowing down to your heart chakra, solar plexus chakra and sacral chakra, and then finishing up with your root chakra.

As this continues, visualize your breath moving out from each chakra into every part of your body, bringing life-force energy into all your cells and the spaces in between. Breathe in spaciousness and breathe out stuckness, limited beliefs, tension, and anything else ready to be loosened and expelled.

Continue taking slow, deep in-breaths, followed by gentle out-breaths, releasing heaviness. The breath is fluid and flows unobstructed with infinite ease. There is no need to hold on or be on high alert, scanning for danger. This practice is just an invitation to go deeper and let it all go, bringing life-force energy to your whole being. Breathe harmoniously, one breath at a time.

After a few minutes of breathing this way, close your eyes and be still for a while. Soak in the pleasant sensations inside of you. Continue sensing your in-breath as it revitalizes you and clears your chakras, breathing out what no longer serves you. Let's check in for a moment. What are you experiencing? What feels different inside of you now? Hopefully, it feels good in some way. I find this an excellent way to reboot my system, release stuck energy, and fill the entirety of my being with invigorating life-force energy.

In addition to breathing into our golden central channel and chakras, it's also fabulously healing and loving to direct our breath to our physical sensations. By this, I mean any parts of the body that are numb, tense, tight, in pain, or calling for our attention in some way.

Change can happen quickly when we channel our loving, tender breath to parts of our bodies that are feeling uncomfortable. It's commonplace for the intensity of the sensation to reduce significantly, sometimes disappearing altogether. We can supercharge this experience by visualizing breathing in specific essences, like relaxation, gentleness, or acceptance. Choose the ones that you sense will be most helpful for you.

Give it a go. Play with this approach. Breathe into any areas experiencing discomfort, pain, or feeling out of sorts. It's as if we're saying, *It's okay, my love. I'm right here. I'm listening to you. I've got you.* It's an incredibly powerful way to love ourselves in the present moment. It's best to release any expectations or attachment to the outcome and stay curious, allowing our awareness to show us what's possible. All we need to do is relax and let our life-force energy saturate our being.

Okay, we've discovered that breathing into sensations in the physical body helps us feel better. So does directing our breath into the core of intense, difficult emotions that arise. When experiencing strong emotions with low energetic frequencies like anger, fear, sadness, guilt, despair, or a potent mix of several emotions entangled together, it's an act of self-love to bring our breath directly to the emotion.

Our human instinct is to avoid feeling painful emotions. Overall, we prefer to experience emotions that feel great rather than unpleasant. We often try to ignore or suppress the ones that don't feel good, and distracting ourselves by watching TV, eating unhealthy food, obsessing about sex, excessive shopping, drinking alcohol, or taking recreational drugs.

When we try to push down or avoid feeling the difficult stuff, sometimes their energy escapes from us in different ways. We can act directly from that intense emotion, from our pain, by screaming and shouting at someone or blaming others, lashing out, and taking it out on the world in some shape or form. And we can project it onto others, where we see those emotions in them but cannot see them in ourselves.

What I'm about to share may seem radical to some of you. The opportunity always exists to do the opposite of what we most want to do in challenging times. Instead of avoiding the difficult emotions, we can give them our full, loving attention, and breathe into the very heart of them. Embrace them with a compassionate heart rather than bolting from them out of fear.

To enhance your understanding, I'll use the emotion of hopelessness as an example, but please replace it with whatever feeling is present for you. Take some deep breaths, breathing out any tension, before gently asking yourself where that emotion (e.g., hopelessness) is located inside you. Do a scan of your body and discover where it resides. Is it in your throat, heart, chest, jaw, hips, stomach, or lower back? Quite honestly, it can be stored anywhere in your body. If this is a struggle for you, it can be helpful to ask yourself, "If I did know where this hopelessness was in me, where would it be?" and then notice what comes to mind. Your body will let you know, if you give it a chance to show you. The response may be subtle, obvious, or somewhere in between. Trust the answer you receive.

Then, with no agenda other than taking great care of yourself, send your in-breath to that part of your body, right into the emotion. Every emotion has its own energy field. Breathe into the center of the energy field of the emotion and ignore all stories and thoughts about the emotion or what has happened. That includes who you believe is to blame, what happened to make you feel this way, how things always go wrong for you, etc. It also includes any inner commentary about the sensation of the emotion, how much it hurts, or that it will never go away. Treat the story like a cloud passing through the sky: detach from it and watch it without touching it. Take your focus away from any mental activity and place your awareness on breathing into the emotion and breathing out whatever is ready to be resolved.

Sometimes, the emotion is felt everywhere in the body, a general feeling that is impossible to pinpoint. Should this happen, breathe into the core of the feeling without needing to know its precise location.

Resistance can surface as we breathe into an emotion, preventing us from experiencing the feeling fully. Resistance is how our egoic personalities attempt to protect us. It can be intense and difficult to budge. The ego falsely believes that avoiding painful emotions will keep us safe somehow. At the root of resistance, fear usually exists: fear of feeling emotions, fear of survival, and fear of the past, present, and future. The best way to deal with resistance and the associated fear is to be gentle and compassionate, acknowledging and welcoming it. Speak lovingly and directly to the resistance, saying thank you for trying to protect you. Reassure the resistance by letting it know your adult self will always look after you, keeping you safe, so it can relax and rest. Resistance will usually lessen or disappear when we speak with it in this manner, helping you to gain access to the energy field of the emotion.

It's important to do this without any attachment or expectation of feeling better. We simply meet what is present and accept it. When we come to it freshly each time, not knowing what will happen, we tend to discover that our emotions lessen or vanish completely.

A quick word on belly breathing, also known as diaphragmatic breathing. It's a fabulous way to stimulate our vagus nerve, activating our parasympathetic nervous system, which relaxes us deeply. I don't know about you, but I rarely let my stomach muscles relax. I'm often holding them in to some degree, using my core muscles to support my spine or make myself look slightly slimmer! Belly breathing is most effective when our abdominal muscles are slack, so relaxing any tight muscles before we begin is a good idea. Imagine the air moving down through your body to your belly. Then relax as you exhale, without forcing the air out. Continue for a few minutes, and that's it! Belly breathing is brilliant when you need a quick way to relax and reduce stress levels.

Masses of information exist on various breathing techniques, on the internet and in print. Some approaches stimulate us, some help us to focus, while others encourage deep relaxation. Over the years, I've tried several techniques to increase focus and calm my nervous system, but I'm particularly fond of the 4:8 pattern: Breathing in through your nose for a count of four and exhaling through your mouth for a count of eight. In effect, your exhalation is twice as long as your inhalation. I learned this easy and effective breathing pattern many years ago during an NLP training course.

The great news is that just a few minutes of breathing this way leads to profound relaxation and a sense of expansiveness. It facilitates letting go of persistent, unhelpful thoughts and creates a sense of delicious rest and relief.

Because the 4:8 breathing technique is so effective, I've taught it to hundreds of friends and clients. It's my go-to approach to help people unwind and access their intuition. Sometimes, it takes people a while to adjust to the longer exhalation. They can feel like they've run out of air too quickly. If that happens to you, try gently exhaling smaller amounts of air as you count to eight. You'll soon pick it up.

As someone prone to being anxious and easily stressed, I find the 4:8 breathing technique extremely powerful at quickly relaxing my nervous system. In a calmer state, I can think more clearly, hear my intuition, and make better decisions. It's my saving grace when I get stressed, overwhelmed, or upset about something. I whip it out at the dentist, at medical visits, when I'm running late, stuck in slow traffic, while cooking up a storm for big family gatherings, before, during, and after difficult conversations, and in many other circumstances.

Last year, I got a routine mammogram and ultrasound. I've had callbacks before, which is always stressful. Like many of us, I know quite a few women who've had breast cancer. Some died; some are still alive. A dear soul sister recently underwent breast cancer treatment. So, these appointments make me somewhat anxious. During the ultrasound, the technician took ages as she probed around in a couple of different areas of my left breast. She remained silent as she did so, and her silence got me worried. I assumed she would tell me if everything looked okay. She kept returning to the same area. I felt my stress levels rising, so I started my 4:8 breathing, letting go of the scary stories I was telling myself. I breathed in the essences of calm and *Love* and exhaled stress and tension. It made a massive difference as I lay there; I felt peace descending all around and within me. The 4:8 pattern enabled me to create a welcome distance from the thoughts and beliefs flying around and continually brought me back to the present moment. When she finished the scan, she told me it had taken so long because she'd been measuring existing cysts as requested by the doctor. It turned out that my scary stories were unfounded. One cyst had disappeared, and the others had reduced significantly. Adopting the 4:8 pattern really helped me to calm down during that highly charged moment.

I encourage you to give this breathing technique a go to see if it works well for you. You may have your own preferred breathing approaches. Use whatever methods feel good to you and bring you relief. It's easy to forget to use these exceptionally powerful breathing tools when we need them the most. So, this chapter is a loving nudge to remind you to use them when you need to create inner calm.

In 2023, one of my dear friends, Lourdes, told me about a powerful awakening experience she'd had through breathwork while on a spiritual retreat in Tulum, Mexico. It was the first time I'd heard about breathwork. Being a naturally inquisitive person, I was keen to experience it for

myself. A few weeks later, while attending a deeply meditative sound bath at the Hummingbird Healing Center in
Westport, I met a lovely Shamanic practitioner, Katie, with
*Love* and vitality blazing out of her eyes. She told me about
an upcoming holotropic breathwork event at her healing
center. It was a different type of breathwork from the one
Lourdes had raved about; nonetheless, I was eager to experience it, so I signed up!

The morning of the breathwork event arrived. There
were about eight women in the room, and excitement and
nervousness saturated the air. Our breathwork facilita-
tor, Bianca, showed up in a brown cowboy hat and a black
leather jacket with fringes underneath the arms. She was
loudly enthusiastic with a cheeky glint in her eyes. She
swore like a sailor, had a superb sense of humor, and
exuded *Love.*

If you're unfamiliar with holotropic breathwork, I'll
gallop through the fundamentals. You begin by setting an
intention for your session. Then you lie on a yoga mat without anything beneath your head and cover yourself with
blankets. With a playlist of music blasting out, you follow
a specific breathing pattern for about twenty-five minutes. There are two stages to the inhalation. The first part
involves breathing in about 80 percent of your breath into
your belly, feeling the belly rise, and then, without exhaling, you inhale the remaining 20 percent of your breath
into your chest, feeling it expand. As you exhale, you relax
and release the air from your body without force. Both the
inhalation and the exhalation take place through your

mouth, for the entire twenty-five minutes.

It's a heck of a workout and can become highly laborious. People respond differently to breathwork, and the experience tends to vary every time you do it. It can produce crying, laughing, coughing, shaking, numbness, tingling, temporary paralysis — anything goes! It can be a noisy and chaotic experience. When the music ends, you're guided to scream at the top of your lungs and then laugh out loud before falling into silence in savasana — also called the corpse pose — for around ten minutes. Then, you are gently brought back into full waking consciousness.

During the breathwork, I felt intense tingling throughout my whole body, and in savasana, I had a strange sensation that something outside of me was breathing my body. My breathing got deeper, faster, and more forceful, like a steam train, and I couldn't slow it down. My mouth started making strange twitching movements as if desperately holding back tears, which was confusing because I was unaware of any strong emotions. Then, tears started pouring from my eyes. At that moment, I sensed that I was fully surrendered to the Divine. Gratitude and *Love* flooded my body. In my mind's eye, I spoke with the Divine, asking it to use me as a conduit for the benefit of all. I offered myself to the Divine in entirety, to be of service to humanity and to share *Love* with the world. Energy surged through my whole being.

Wiping away the tears from the side of my face, I sat up slowly, feeling very trancey and in a vastly altered state. I looked at everyone in the room, all total strangers, and felt tremendous *Love* for every single one of them. I proclaimed, "I just want to hug you all!". Several of them came over and hugged me. What a blessed moment. My heart was wide open.

I was flying so high that I remarked to the woman beside me, "Now I have to go to the supermarket?! How the hell am I going to manage that?!" All I wanted to do was lie down on the grass and merge with nature. It was a sublime experience, an intense, loving fragrance that lingered for several days.

Since then, I've experienced breathwork many times. It's a magnificent way to strengthen our connection to the Divine and our intuition, and to boost our ability to love ourselves.

Profound heart healings have occurred during my other breathwork trips. I've experienced the letting go of deeper layers of hurt and rejection and peeling away more of who I am not, gradually revealing more of my light and raising my vibration one breath at a time. My guides showed up in these sessions, imparting loving support as they held me with such tenderness. They kissed my forehead in the gentlest of ways, reassuring me that all was well even though life seemed overwhelming and chaotic. They lovingly reminded me that the power lies in the stillness rather than the words we speak. It's our intention and presence that create lasting transformation.

In this chapter you've likely noticed that I've often referred to the effectiveness of inhaling specific essences when you need some assistance. If you're stressed, overwhelmed, or in an emotional storm, pause and think of what you'd like to experience instead. How do you want to feel? Which essences would be most beneficial? This is not a complete list, but here are some suggestions: courage, safety, confidence, calm, clarity, compassion, forgiveness, comfort, trust, patience, surrender, or *Love*.

Choose whatever resonates strongly for you. As you breathe in, visualize filling yourself with your chosen quality. As you exhale, gently release what has been troubling you. Take one essence at a time, completely saturating yourself with it before breathing out the tension and unwanted energies from your body and energy field. It feels outrageously good to do this.

All in all, conscious breathing is free and easy to adopt. All we need to do is remind ourselves to use it on our journey into truly loving and looking after ourselves.

# 9

# A GENTLER PACE OF LIFE

Suddenly, we found ourselves face to face with an enormous, majestic bull elephant, teeming with strength and hormones. The air crackled with his powerful energy. He seemed agitated and angry as he displayed his dominance towards us. Clouds of sandy-colored dust billowed up from the ground, kicked up into the air by his sudden, aggressive movements. Terrified, we stopped in our tracks and were rooted to the spot.

James, Jess, Josh, and I were on a family safari holiday in 2017, deep in Kruger Park, South Africa.

We'd been on several game drives during our trip, viewing wildlife from the safety of a safari jeep. Our early morning drives were peppered with drinking rooibos tea and munching on rusks — a traditional South African dry biscuit meant for dunking in hot drinks. We soaked in jaw-droppingly gorgeous sunsets on our evening drives as we sipped sundowners and nibbled on nuts.

To make our experience infinitely more exciting and a little less comfortable, James organized a walking safari for us.

So, there we were, four Linnetts walking in single file through the African bush, with an armed tracker at the front and an armed safari guide at the rear of the line. We were assured that the guns would only be used to scare off wildlife should things get a little out of hand.

Before we set out on our walking safari, our guides thoroughly prepped us on essential safety rules to follow. They wanted to avoid encountering certain animals at close quarters, and a young bull elephant was high on the list because they can be extremely dangerous, aggressive, and unpredictable towards humans on foot.

The glorious bull elephant stood about one-hundred feet in front of our walking party. Our guides started to make calming yet assertive noises towards him. The elephant's ears flapped, and he threw his head around and emitted almighty angry and threatening roars, warning us of his tempestuous hormonal status.

All the while, the elephant kept his eyes on us — vulnerable, squashable humans who just stood there and watched him right back.

Silence from the Linnetts, that's remarkable for a start! Also of interest was that I can be a fierce, protective mummy bear where my kids are concerned. But standing there, frozen to the spot, with nowhere to run and no point in trying, my outrageously protective patterns were noticeably absent.

Even though fear was pumping through my body, something deep inside me knew to be still, be calm, and breathe deeply. It was as if time stood still; well, to be more accurate, it felt like we were outside of time as we observed the elephant.

The four of us remained silent as the guides continued communicating with the elephant, gently but firmly encouraging him to move on. We stood in a line in the dusty, sandy bush, facing the elephant as he continued to vocalize how disgruntled he was at our presence.

To my great surprise, I felt calm descend inside of me. I continued to breathe deeply, imagining myself joining with the elephant in our hearts, speaking to him from the core of my being. Honoring him, respecting him, and admiring him.

I found myself fully present in the moment, feeling the heat on my face, the ground underneath my feet, and the smell of the dirt, with my senses keenly aware of the whole situation. My inner world had slowed down, and my thoughts had vanished. Stillness pervaded. In this calm state, I took in every single aspect of this incredible elephant, connecting with him and respecting his life-force energy and magnificence.

A few minutes later, our guides succeeded in persuading him to move on, and he trundled off on his way. They were visibly relieved that we had escaped unscathed from our surprise encounter.

This incredible moment was one of the greatest gifts in my life, where fear subsided as calm descended. Being still and quiet, connecting with nature, breathing as one, hearts beating as one ... while time stood still.

I grapple with slowing down. It's one of my continuing areas of inner growth. I seem to rush around a lot, find it hard to sit still, and often have a busy mind that tends to overanalyze everything. How about you?

It can take enormous effort and determination to shift these deeply ingrained patterns. People can be stubbornly reluctant to take a more relaxed pace.

The truth is that slowing down our bodies and racing minds creates powerful benefits for our health and lives in general. At a gentler pace, we can better look after ourselves, nurture our relationships, show up authentically, and connect with our deeper selves.

Intuition flows much more freely when we slow down and tune into our inner environment. At a slower pace, the opportunity arises to give ourselves the time and space we need to open up to difficult emotions that we may be unaware of or have been avoiding. Meeting our intense emotions is the doorway to experiencing lasting self-love.

Let's examine some of the detrimental aspects of the fast-paced societies that many of us reside in.

You might be tempted to skip this part because it may be uncomfortable to read. If that's the case, I encourage you to keep reading.

Reading about some of the challenges may help you identify whether living at an accelerated pace is negatively impacting your own life.

Notice how your body responds as you read, without analyzing your realizations or judging yourself. If it doesn't feel great, take it as a sign that maybe your body is nudging you to make some healthy changes.

There is a natural tendency for us to avoid what doesn't feel good and focus on things that feel lovely instead. By doing this, we miss out on the richness of the human experience, of meeting and accepting the totality of life — the highs, the lows, and everything in between.

If we truly desire freedom and peace of mind, it's essential to face all aspects of our human adventure — the good, the bad, and the ugly. Spiritual maturity develops when we meet and experience all of life.

I'll discuss the status quo first, before sharing some thoughts on creating a slower pace and a more loving approach in our lives.

Life is outrageously fast-paced these days, and it can be an ongoing struggle trying to keep up. Many of us are experiencing unbearable levels of stress, anxiety, overwhelm, and loneliness. On some levels, we're accustomed to feeling like this, as if it's the norm. And so, we rarely pause or slow down long enough to question it or do much to alleviate the detrimental impacts on our well-being. In many instances, we're just trying to keep going, keeping our heads above water, with fear of failure snapping at our heels.

Internet access has allowed us to tap into the opinions and ideas of countless people, many of whom claim to be experts in their fields. The volume of information coming our way can overload our nervous systems, and conflicting advice can generate considerable confusion. It can be tough to know who to listen to or trust.

Believing we need to make rapid decisions or get the

facts NOW, the easiest solution often seems to be listening to and acting upon the ideas of others, rather than tuning into our own intuitive guidance. We regularly do this even when their input doesn't feel good, bypassing our own internal compass and blithely following their suggestions.

In doing so, we repeatedly hand over our power to others, dismissing our own inner wisdom and mistrusting our intuition. Over time, this can contribute to a fragmentation in our energetic being, which gets stronger and more deeply fractured as we continue to believe others to be the authority.

When I wanted to chat with my friends as a teenager, I had to call them on the home phone, which seems so archaic now. As the phone cable was connected to the wall, that involved chatting in the hallway, running my fingers over the leaf-textured privacy glass surrounding the front door. I hogged the home phone for hours as we chatted and chuckled about boys and friends, as well as planning our outfits and social activities for the coming weekend.

There was a cut-off point in the evening, after which it was deemed unacceptable to call someone up, except for genuine emergencies. We were uncontactable for many hours in the day while away from our landlines, which freed up time for us to get bored — a lost art form, in my opinion, as it often gives rise to bright ideas and magnificent insights. It also gave us more time for reflection and helped us slow down the pace of life, giving our nervous systems a chance to rest and recuperate.

These days, as you know, we're available 24/7. Texting

and messaging are currently the predominant modes of communication. We can contact someone whenever we want and send emails in the middle of the night if we feel so inclined. Many of us check our phones obsessively to see if we have any new messages. Our email inboxes are fit to burst as the emails pile in each day. Most focus on selling something to us rather than personal messages from people who matter to us.

Social media can be a valuable tool and a lot of fun, but it can also adversely affect us. It's outrageously addictive, like a piece of cheese to a mouse. Every time we see a great post or receive a "like" or a comment, we get a dopamine hit, and that high we experience keeps us hooked.

It's easy to lose track of time as we scroll through social media posts. An hour can pass in the blink of an eye, leaving us wondering what on earth happened! Add to that the obsessive checking of how many people have liked our posts or commented, and eagerly switching between apps just in case we miss out on something juicy.

Far too easily, we compare our lives to the seemingly perfect existences of others, ending up feeling dissatisfied with our bodies, wealth, careers, or relationships.

Social media usage can be a powerful way of distracting ourselves from our own realities and can weaken our relationship with our inner selves.

Our use of technology, in its various forms, dominates many of our lives. It can contribute to an overstimulated, distracted mind that finds it hard to settle and focus. With less time to spend on the things that matter most to us, we can feel a deeply uncomfortable time crunch.

Do you watch or read the news? News outlets tend to churn out events in a fear-based, sensational fashion to attract viewers or readers. They rarely give us considered or objective views of current affairs. Catching up with the news can be stressful and depressing, contributing to a racing mind and a general sense of hopelessness, unease, and fear.

The last thing I want to share with you is the obsession with "doing" rather than "being." I've lived in America for eighteen years at this point, and I've noticed there is an unhealthy addiction in this country to doing, doing, doing, constantly being busy, and overscheduling. It seems as though being busy earns you a badge of honor. Many hurtle along on a fast track that they believe, on some level, will enable them to get ahead or be successful in some way. Even children's lives are caught up in this insanity. They learn this way of living from an early age. It's exhausting and depleting when we get lost in the frenzy of "doing."

Slowing down, connecting with others in meaningful ways, resting, doing absolutely nothing, and simply being are often regarded as unimportant, lazy, or unproductive.

As you read through that, did anything jump out at you about your own life that might require a little tweaking? If so, you're in good company; most of us need a little nudge in this department.

What kind of speed do you notice inside of you right

now? Are you primarily a calm person, or do you regularly feel on edge, operating at a fast pace with a scattered, busy mind?

My inner world can run extremely fast in energetic terms. Sometimes, that's because I receive massive energy downloads from my guides or the Divine. They can last for days before subsiding. This rapid pace also occurs when I'm upset, stressed, or overwhelmed.

Many of us who've had dysfunctional childhoods or experienced trauma in our lives tend to feel on edge and operate at a supersonic pace, like a hamster high on sugar, whizzing around on its wheel. It's the fight, flight, freeze response at work in our bodies. This stress reaction can also make it tough to sit still for long, and we find ourselves wriggling around, tapping our feet and constantly changing position to get comfortable.

Let's move on to some important benefits of slowing down:

- Helps us to be in the present moment, catching ourselves when we're caught up in the past or preoccupied with the future
- Improves our health by reducing stress, anxiety, and overwhelm
- Improves the quality of our sleep (mainly by slowing down the pace inside of us)

- Enhances our ability to sense the rhythm of life through Mother Nature
- Makes it easier to connect with our intuition
- Encourages gratitude to flow more freely
- Helps us to effectively interrupt unwanted patterns of behavior, which helps us to live happier lives
- Improves our relationship with ourselves because we are better able to take care of our physical, emotional, and mental needs
- Encourages deep and authentic connections with others
- Enhances our ability to be great listeners
- Allows us to notice our emotions more readily, and clear dense energy out of our bodies and energy fields
- Helps us to decipher the signals and messages that our bodies send us

In bringing all the above together, we are better able to love ourselves when we slow the heck down.

That's a long list of fabulous benefits!

Most of us find it challenging to slow down, partly because society encourages overwhelm and a fast pace. In attempting to slow down, we find ourselves swimming against an incessant, forceful current, often believing it's easier to go with the flow than break out of the norm.

Go easy on yourself as you start to make some changes

in the realm of slowing down — one small step at a time. I encourage you to celebrate all your successes, however small they may seem.

Hopefully, a smattering of my words will inspire you to find strategies that work well for you. If something doesn't work, slip into creative mode, think laterally, and find an approach that does.

It seems to me that there are two aspects of slowing down, and they are interrelated. We can slow down our physical bodies and we can slow down our internal world. Easing up on one of them often tends to calm the other, too, but not always.

I tend to scurry about, so I bump into things regularly. Last year, I broke two toes in succession. On both occasions I was dashing about without being fully present in the moment. It took the second break for me to really take heed of the message to slow down substantially.

The fractured toes forced me to rest and stay home for a while. Broken toes are surprisingly painful, and I was inactive for about five months in total. I sense it was the Universe's way of getting me to sit down and crack on with writing this book. In all honesty, I'd been distracting myself rather a lot up to that point.

With all my toes intact, I now move around more slowly and deliberately, noticing how my feet feel on the ground. I focus on the present moment and am much more aware of my surroundings.

Being in the present moment doesn't require us to be stationary. My overactive, scattered mind settles down when I'm exercising outdoors. In fact, I often receive valuable information downloads from my guides and brilliant intuitive insights when walking at the beach or cycling.

Years ago, I used to push my body hard while exercising. A typical day involved briskly walking the dog a couple of miles, tough core barre classes, or playing tennis, followed by swimming forty lengths. I'm exhausted remembering that! My body started to get injured. It was trying to communicate with me, but I wasn't listening.

It took a rather dramatic injury during tennis practice for me to realize it was time to look inward and understand what was happening. My body was letting me know that it needed me to slow down. Initially, I was extremely reluctant to do this and wanted to push through it because I loved the endorphin high.

I ended up listening, though, and I made some big changes. These days, I walk the dog for a couple of miles a day, cycle a couple of times a week, boogie for short spells, and do some gentle Pilates or yoga.

It was tough letting go of my addiction to moving quickly and pushing my body. However, I'm so glad I listened to my body and decided to care for its needs lovingly. Changing my exercise habits had a delightful knock-on effect of creating a slower pace on the inside.

Do you tend to juggle too much at once? I do. Countless times in my life, I've felt weighed down by the tasks at hand, having said yes to way too many things. With my inner world spinning out of control, I get overwhelmed and lack the clarity to see what steps I need to take to resolve my situation.

When it all feels like too much, and we're buckling under the weight of it all, it's time to take a step back. It's helpful to rise high above the details of the overwhelm, like an eagle soaring in the sky, overseeing the whole situation, taking some deep breaths of clarity and calm, and breathing out tension, agitation, and stress.

From this higher vantage point, a clearer understanding often emerges, calm descends, and guidance about what to do next often appears in our mind's eye. We may receive a sense of the very next step, however small.

Sometimes, we gain clarity on which balls to drop or put lovingly to one side for a while and which projects or tasks are truly lit up for us to focus on at that moment in time.

When I was in the mix of redesigning and rewriting my website, writing my book, uncertain about how to get my book published, in the early stages of getting my YouTube channel up and running, and dealing with my dad's estate issues after his death, with grief lingering around, I was stressed out and struggling to gain clarity. It took an insightful friend to lovingly take me up to those heights, soaring above the storm, to see that the key thing to focus on was writing my book.

Sometimes, it takes a wise soul to nudge us in the right direction when we're in the thick of it. And that's okay. At times like this, remember the eagle view and give it a go for yourself. Failing that, make a date with a perceptive friend!

Do you create avoidable stress in your life? I do sometimes. I love solving Sudoku puzzles on my phone. I used to have the built-in stop clock counting down as I figured out the number placements, watching the seconds tick by.

After a while, I noticed the constant time pressure was stressing me out. It was so unnecessary! My inner world was running at a million miles an hour. I realized I kept darting my eyes to the timer as I grappled with the puzzle. My competitive streak was constantly trying to better my time, and I was hard on myself if I was slow to solve it.

After a few months, I switched the stop clock off. That simple step helped me slow down and enjoy the puzzle instead of thinking I needed to hurry up. It was a quick change that made an enormous difference.

Does my Sudoku story highlight ways you might be creating unnecessary time pressures for yourself? If so, perhaps consider some ways you can be kinder to yourself by creating a slower pace. They might be blindingly obvious, like mine was.

Making changes on such a small level may seem trivial, but don't be fooled. These little adjustments contribute to significant improvements in our overall well-being. And they feel manageable, so we have minimal resistance to doing them.

What are some simple solutions to support you in living your life more harmoniously?

Breathe deeply. If you aren't a believer yet, trust me when I say deep breathing is incredibly effective at slowing us down internally. When we're spinning quickly, it makes a massive difference, rapidly bringing calm to our reality.

Other brilliant ways to relax our nervous systems and

encourage relaxation are meditation and quiet time.

We reap the greatest rewards by incorporating them into our ongoing daily self-care routine. Even super-short sessions can activate the relaxation response. I find it most effective when I meditate a few times a day for about ten to fifteen minutes rather than one longer stint.

When I slip out of this meditation habit, I notice that my inner world speeds up again.

Mindfulness is exceptionally powerful at bringing us to the present moment. It keeps us from getting stuck in the past or worrying or dreaming about the future. Simple things like wriggling a toe or twitching your nose or feeling the air temperature on your face work wonders. Combined with deep breathing, mindfulness always slows down and calms my busy, overanalyzing mind, creating relief and inner space.

Taking it to the next level, if you're feeling courageous and up for a challenge, set aside time to do absolutely nothing. Perhaps start with an hour, then move to half days and whole days now and then. No reading, TV, or phones — you get the idea — nothing, although being in nature and gentle walking are allowed.

Listening to beautiful, soothing music can help us to fall into a gentler internal space. And for that matter, singing and humming are fabulous gateways for shifting into a calmer, more harmonious state.

The next idea is obvious but often one of the most challenging suggestions to embrace: reducing TV, phone, internet, and social media time. A couple of years ago, my daughter took a break from social media for a few months. She deleted the apps from her phone and shared that it made a massive difference to her, creating more time in her day to do things that made her feel good about herself.

When she returned to social media, her relationship with it had changed for the better. She now limits her phone time and maintains a healthy perspective while scrolling.

I've made a few changes with my phone usage. For a start, I switch it off when walking, preferring to be present with my surroundings. My phone is off while I'm exercising and sleeping. When writing, I put my phone on "Do Not Disturb" to help me focus.

When it dawned on me that I don't have to respond to messages immediately, I felt less pressured and more relaxed. Quite simply, there is no urgency. I get to decide when I'm ready to respond or if a reply is even necessary.

I feel noticeably calmer having made these adjustments. I check my phone less, knowing that most things are not pressing. Regularly unplugging from my phone is a way of honoring my well-being.

Moving onto the news. Ask yourself, and be honest here, how often do you watch or read the news each day?

I limit the time I spend reading online news because I tend to check events too frequently. A restless hunger compels me to find out what's going on in the world. Instead of satiating my hunger, it contributes to a stressed and unsettled energy in me.

During the 2020 presidential election, this compulsion became obsessive and had a very negative impact on my inner state. Needing to make a change, I took a news holiday, which lasted for several weeks and did me a world of good. I felt happier, more content, and at ease.

Watching American news on TV was too stressful for me. Their fear-mongering approach, full of violent crime reports, made me anxious. So, I stopped watching and don't miss it at all. Reading the news online is much kinder to my nervous system.

Getting out in nature is good for us on numerous levels. It encourages a gentler pace inside of us. And we don't have to visit an exotic location to benefit. Wherever we live, we can get outside, notice the birds and the plants, and feel the weather on our faces. I love it when I get drenched in the rain. It's so liberating — delighting my inner child and making me smile inside and out. Covered in rain, I feel connected to nature rather than separate from it.

Powerful ways to benefit from Mother Nature's soothing and healing energies include grounding ourselves by putting our bare feet on the grass, sand, or soil, or by getting them wet in the ocean. Caress trees and run your hands through the grass! I often sit on the beach meditating with my hands in the sand. It's blissful — slowing everything down inside, creating blessed harmony.

Are you an avid list maker? I always have a list on the go. I inherited that from my mum. She is the queen of list-making!

It's easy to feel stressed or demoralized at the end of the day when we haven't finished as many tasks on our list as we'd intended to.

I've made some healthy changes to my list-making habit. I used to be unrealistic about what was humanly possible to achieve in one day! I've taken that pressure off myself and now carefully consider my priorities. I put fewer jobs on my daily to-do list, and I'm happy to reschedule tasks without feeling like a failure. I see it as creating a healthy balance in my life, and I'm no longer a slave to my list.

A great tip I've learned the hard way is to break down big tasks into smaller, more manageable ones. It might seem obvious to you, but I wasn't doing this.

Did you know we get a dopamine hit whenever we tick something off our list? That hit is a welcome boost that has a cumulative effect throughout the day. The more tasks we tick off, no matter the importance, the better we feel about ourselves.

When faced with an overwhelming list of to-dos, rather than believing that we must do them all — or something terrible will befall us — we can take a fresh approach.

Take a moment to reassess your list; some tasks may not need immediate attention, or perhaps even any at all. Reschedule any non-urgent items to create welcome space for yourself, or let go of those that you decide are unnecessary.

For the rest of the tasks that genuinely need attention, you can determine who needs to perform them. The number of times I've taken on jobs that I could easily have delegated to others is countless. Emptying the dishwasher, nipping to the grocery store, and making dinner are perfect examples. We can end up doing too much when we buy into false beliefs like *I'm the only one who can do it well;* or *No one supports me, so I have to do it all by myself.*

Sometimes, instead of delegating tasks individually, it helps to share responsibilities within a group. For example, when my kids were younger and living at home, I partici- pated in carpools with other parents to transport our kids to and from activities and school drop-offs. This group effort made an enormous difference to me — freeing up a tremendous amount of time by taking turns rather than handling every trip on my own.

It's also helpful to remember that to ease our load, we can hire external assistance, whether it's fixing a leaking faucet or writing sales copy for our business projects.

When faced with a task that we don't want to do — that we'd rather avoid at all costs — we can get creative and make the experience more pleasant. I don't enjoy ironing. I tend to put it off until the clothes are bone dry. I've found that when I plan my time well and listen to interesting podcasts, online courses, or audiobooks while ironing, it actually turns into a fairly pleasant experience.

Another way of dealing with a task that we aren't keen on is to do something lovely for ourselves afterward. When I'm going for a mammogram, I decide before my appoint- ment what I can do later that same day to put a smile on my face. Depending on my mood or the weather, I might take a long bath infused with rose essential oil, pop to the beach, or watch an episode of *The Great British Bake-Off.*

I use a few tools to help me slow down and switch off my stress response. My current favorite is a large Tibetan singing bowl. I lie down, place it on my torso and strike it with the mallet. Soothing, delicious vibrations spread through my body, releasing tension and overwhelm. I'm also a big fan of using tuning forks, crystals, and infrared light technology, all of which promote relaxation, pain relief, and healing, helping me rebalance and soften, facilitating a return to homeostasis.

Let's talk about gratitude for a minute. Simply put, slowing down our frantic pace makes it easier to think of things that we are genuinely grateful for. When we take time to connect with what we feel grateful for, *Love* floods our being. Practicing gratitude is a wonderful way to care for and love ourselves.

In contrast, if we treat expressing gratitude as a rote exercise, naming what we're grateful for and rushing through the process, we miss out on the powerful gifts that true gratitude offers to us.

It's particularly valuable to think of what we're thankful for when we're struggling in life — even if all we can manage is "I'm still breathing" or feeling grateful for the blue sky, rain, a cup of tea, a bed to sleep in, or clean, running water from a faucet. You get the idea. And if your body is in a state of dis-ease, focus on the body parts that are in good health, like your pinky toe or the tip of your nose. Be thankful for what is working well.

This practice of "not that but this," thinking not about

the problem but what we are thankful for, is a potent and effective way to redirect our negativity to something supportive and loving. But for it to truly benefit us, we need to be sincere about what we're grateful for.

Perhaps you'd like to start a gratitude practice or rekindle one if it's fallen by the wayside. Find a way of bringing it into your life that aligns with you. Always remember that you are the only expert on you. Be guided by what feels good to you.

I often express my gratitude to the Divine at bedtime or first thing in the morning. I also find myself deeply moved by gratitude when I am outside, marveling at the magnificence of nature.

When we forget to use our slowing-down tools and habits, it's common for our agitation and stress levels to increase.

At these times, it's essential to be kind to ourselves and focus on making some changes to calm everything down again. We are human, after all, and it's to be expected that we have times when we are in the flow and doing a great job of looking after ourselves and then other moments when it all goes off track. And that's okay.

Be gentle with yourself if you find yourself back at one thousand miles an hour. Simply notice how you feel, regard it as feedback, and then do one simple thing that helps you regain some balance and inner tranquility.

I think of it as a process of ongoing readjustments.

Play with taking a gentler pace, and you'll deepen your relationship with yourself and enhance your capacity to love yourself unconditionally.

# 10

# BINGO! THERE IT IS!

It is in the stillness and silence of the mind that we discover our true essence and recognize ourselves as *Love*. Even if we experience this just for a moment, the game is over. We can't continue withholding *Love* from ourselves in such a determined fashion. We find that even though we might continue to believe ourselves to be damaged, unworthy, or unlovable in some ways, when we experience our true selves as *Love*, the truth is we are instantly and permanently transformed. From that moment onwards, it becomes futile to attempt to deny or diminish our true nature. We can no longer tell ourselves with conviction the same old stories of suffering.

It gets to a point where it becomes rather amusing when we lapse into unloving thoughts about ourselves because we can't take our suffering too seriously anymore. Our tales of woe just don't seem to stick in the same way as they used to, which can be rather unsatisfying. And we begin to overhear, with increasing ease, the repetitive stories we keep telling ourselves. All of this creates space between our mind chatter and deeper selves, which strengthens our ability to realize that our thoughts are not necessarily based in reality.

In a nutshell, stillness and silence have transformed

my life. Meeting Gangaji, my spiritual teacher, opened the gateways for me to experience undeniable and all-encompassing self-love through silence. She once said, "When you are willing to stop looking for something in thought, you will find everything in silence." I continue to deepen in the truth of that.

Given that this chapter is about silence, you might be assuming that the focus will be on meditation practices. That's what many people equate to silence and stillness. In truth, lots of people find meditation difficult; they wrestle and struggle with silence, believing that they can't meditate. I've had countless conversations with people about meditation troubles over the years. In many cases, they tried a variety of practices and discovered none of them worked well for them, partly because their minds were so scattered and overactive.

It's easy to feel hopeless and disillusioned about meditation when the tools you employ seem to be the very thing getting in your way of reaching a peaceful, centered state. If that resonates with you, know that you're not alone. Keep reading! I have good news for you.

In her YouTube video "Beyond Practice," Gangaji discusses how true freedom can only be reached if we don't do anything for its realization. In her view, if we are willing to stop all practices, including meditation methods, for just one instant, letting go of what we think we need to do to experience bliss, then we discover it's right there.

Aside from meditation practices, there are alternative ways of reaching inner stillness. In my opinion, there is no prescribed approach; it's best to discover what works best for you by trial and error. Some people with noisy, restless minds can only get to a place of stillness and peace through sound. Listening to beautiful music, singing, chanting, and playing instruments, tuning forks, or singing bowls can be very helpful. In the delicious silence that follows the last note played or voiced, the mind can fall into silence and rest.

Walking in nature, whether meandering through woodlands or spending time near lakes, rivers, waterfalls, or the ocean, effortlessly promotes a calm, quiet state. Listening to recorded nature sounds can be marvelous, too. I love listening to recordings of British birdsongs. In a heartbeat, I'm transported to a deep state of relaxation, and my mind falls silent. Ask yourself what would work for you and give it a go, even if it sounds slightly bizarre or ridiculous.

Confession time: I struggled with formal meditation approaches, or at least I did until I gave them up! The ones I tried didn't resonate with me or feel natural. I'd do them for a while before quitting. In the earlier years of my healing journey, guided meditations were invaluable in carrying me to a quiet place inside. They lovingly nudged me to connect with stillness and my inner knowing. I still enjoy listening to meditations from time to time when the person leading knows how to dance with energy and has a soothing, rhythmic voice.

I love recording guided meditations to assist people in making transformations. If you're interested in experiencing them, check out my website information in the "Golden Nuggets" section at the back of this book.

Here's a tip for you when listening to guided meditations: Follow the energy that lies in between and underneath their words. In my opinion, the energy is more important than the words. If you find their pace too fast or slow, let me reassure you that moving at your own speed is okay. Trust the energy and let go of trying to focus intently on their words. Feel free to deviate from the script if you receive images and feelings in your mind's eye that do not align with their cues. Regard their words merely as a jumping-off or access point. And ultimately, if their meditations don't feel like a good fit for you, regardless of how famous they are or how highly your friends recommend them, trust yourself and find someone else that appeals to you. It's worth taking the time to find voices that you resonate with because guided meditations can be a potent transformational tool on your healing journey.

These days, I prefer to experience a profound connection to my inner self in a very simple manner. In a seated position with an elongated spine, I close my eyes, take some slow, deep, gentle breaths, and bring my awareness to my energetic heart — our heart of hearts that lies at the core of our being.

I breathe in and out of my heart space for a while, letting my thoughts come and go without attaching to them. Any noises I hear, like barking dogs, sirens, phone ringing, dishwasher beeping, and other distractions, are my cue to go deeper. That's it. Simple and beautiful.

Wherever I am, peacefulness is available to me in a

heartbeat. I often open to stillness when I'm out and about, although usually with eyes open! I do this in queues in grocery stores, while driving, in airports, at the pharmacy, and in many other situations.

When I'm particularly stressed out, it can be tough to get still, and my mind often fights with me like crazy. I feel like I have ants in my pants, and I can't settle into going inward. At these trickier times, I spend a few minutes dancing, shaking my body, exercising, humming, singing, or shouting to move the energy out before opening to stillness. It's extremely effective and never fails to work.

You might be wondering why stillness and silence are so good for us. Below are a few powerful benefits they bring:

◆ Calm our nervous system, encourage activation of the relaxation response, and allow our bodies to rest and digest, improving our overall health

◆ Reduce our levels of stress, anxiety, and overwhelm

◆ Hone our ability to receive inner guidance from our Higher Self

◆ Enhance clarity and improve our mental focus, facilitating easier and better decision-making

◆ Create a safe sanctuary for unresolved emotions, thoughts, and beliefs to arise and show us what we may have been avoiding in ourselves — bringing us a golden opportunity to love and accept whatever we were previously unaware of or scared to feel

Here's a story for you about the power of silence.

A few years ago, I attended a six-day silent retreat in Salt Spring Island, British Columbia, Canada, with Gangaji. Have you attended silent retreats? If so, you'll be familiar with what tends to happen in all that silence and stillness. For those of you who haven't experienced them, here's a peek inside. Taking this time out of your everyday life, being with yourself fully, with no distractions and no socializing, tends to bring up deep-seated emotions and painful, limiting beliefs. No conversations with others are allowed, and there is nothing to do other than eat, sleep, walk, read spiritual books, and meditate — deafening silence. Meetings with Gangaji take place twice a day, and you're strongly encouraged to take a complete break from all forms of technology for the duration of the retreat.

All that quiet time stirs the pot of what is unresolved within you. It can get exceptionally uncomfortable, and the pressure of what's covering up your radiant self can build up to impressive levels. And that's the reason for the stillness and lack of stimulation. The silence enables what we have been avoiding feeling to rise to the surface so we can become aware of it. If we're willing, we can inquire into the emotions that arise, be present with them, and give whatever shows up our full love and attention. In my experience, honest, genuine inquiry is the most important component of the journey to self-love.

Since my arrival at the retreat center, I'd been feeling

uncomfortable, and it was way more than what silence was unearthing within me. This discomfort was extremely unusual for me at her retreats: I felt grumpy. I'd been allocated accommodation in someone's home within the community, a large wooden cabin in the woods. The owners had vacated to create bedrooms for the students. The day I arrived, I met another woman staying at the same place. As we were both respecting the invitation to be silent, we knew nothing about each other. We smiled at each other, gave each other cheery waves when our paths crossed, and remained silent for the duration of the retreat.

I'd been assigned the small study/family TV room on the ground floor of this cozy, homely, and welcoming cabin. There were bedrooms upstairs, so I assumed others were staying up there besides the woman I'd already met. I didn't bump into them during my time there, and I was so engrossed in my inner world that I didn't question it. My room on the ground floor had no blinds or curtains adorning the window; nothing stopped people from looking in. With great dismay, I saw people strolling past the window. I felt like a tropical fish in a fish tank, except there was no glittery, colorful castle to hide inside to gain privacy. That wasn't going to work for me; I was miserable and knew I was in for a rough week.

A feeling of immense disappointment washed through my body as my eyes landed on the makeshift bed with a thin, unforgiving mattress. If it hadn't taken me so long to get to the retreat center, I might have turned around and gone straight home! But I'd had a long journey that day, with a drive from Connecticut to Newark Airport, a flight to Vancouver, a short flight to Victoria, a taxi ride to a ferry terminal, a ferry to Salt Spring Island, and lastly, a car journey to the retreat center. Salt Spring Island is breath-takingly beautiful; I mean seriously gorgeous; it's very rural and delightfully undeveloped. In lots of ways, it's an escape from the modern world. I had no car, and had I decided to leave, I'd have been stuck for options and faced with an arduous journey back home.

I had no realistic choice except to make the best of it. I know from past experiences that when these unwelcome things happen, they always end up being exceptionally good for me. And relative discomfort always makes me truly appreciate all the wonderful things I have in my everyday life. Even though I was very pissed off at the time, I knew, on some level, the situation would be good for me.

I found some cotton sheets in a closet and devised a clever way to create some window privacy from passers-by. That helped matters, but my goodness, it was an uncomfortable few days. I barely slept a wink on that dreadful bed. To add salt to my wound, the shower produced a pathetic trickle of water. With my long, thick, curly hair, a weak shower was a deal breaker. I was forced to hunt for an alternative and came across a decent shower a ten-minute walk away down a muddy, stony track.

So, I was not in the best of moods, and I was exhausted. I didn't talk to Gangaji's staff about the situation because I didn't want to seem precious or as if I was making a fuss. I didn't want to speak up. As it turned out, my discomfort, exhaustion, and tetchiness were the perfect fuel to throw onto the fire at a silent retreat. It resulted in a deeply buried shameful belief bubbling up to the surface: *I'm unlovable.*

Perhaps you've experienced this: you find yourself doing something your conscious mind is terrified of and screaming at you *NO, don't do it!* and yet, against your better judgment, you feel compelled to do it anyway. When something arises during Gangaji's meetings and retreats for me to discuss or share with her, I get the same sensation bubbling up every single time, without fail. I get this strong sense of being instructed to speak when I'd really rather not; dread mixed with terror floods my cells, my insides go crazy, and my mind says things like *You can't get up there and say that in front of everyone!* In those moments, I'd much rather flee from the meeting hall than get up on the podium with her; nonetheless, it's as if someone has a remote control with a button that raises my hand up high. Sure enough, she chose me. My heart pounded in my chest, my breathing was shallow, and I was intensely anxious and scared as I stood up and made my way to sit in front of Gangaji and about eighty people, acutely aware that thousands of her students would watch the recording.

As I spoke with her, more aspects of my specific blend of unlovability became apparent. It was all news to me; I heard much of it for the first time, even though it emanated from my mouth. This belief, *I'm unlovable*, was complex, and I could see how it impacted numerous areas of my life. It had repeatedly shown up in my relationships. It was one of the most vulnerable moments of my life, sitting up there in conversation with Gangaji, in front of all those people, sharing from the deepest, darkest places inside me. With tears streaming down my face, feeling so ashamed that I believed on some level that I was so unlovable that my own mother had left me as a child. Or so the story went.

With her wise, loving, intuitive nudges and assistance, with her gentle humor and decades of experience, Gangaji guided me effortlessly and gracefully into this unlovability. She said with such kindness, "In this moment, be completely and utterly unlovable." Instead of trying to avoid it, she directed me into the core of unlovability, into the excruciatingly painful, dark, shameful place that lay inside of me. And what happened? What I discovered at the very core of it was *Love* itself. There was no unlovability to be found. Not a trace of it. At the heart of unlovability was *Love*. Vast waves of energy coursed through my body, and the tears that fell were filled with *Love* and gratitude for Gangaji, myself, and the Divine. As I looked into her eyes, *Love* blazed back at me, and I received a jet stream transmission of energy that radiated through her to me; it was undeniable. I was *Love*. Indeed, we are all *Love*.

At that moment, I even had gratitude for the crappy mattress, my makeshift curtains, and my ten-minute walk outside to the shower every day!

The funny thing was, when we came out of silence at the end of the retreat, I got to chat with the woman who stayed in the same house as me. She was lovely and very friendly. I asked her if she'd seen the others staying in our cabin. She told me the other people who were meant to stay there had to move to another home because they were highly allergic to cats. We had a feline companion in the house. In that moment, I discovered that I'd been sleeping on a mattress that was about as comfortable as a door, had barely slept a wink, and had put up with poorly fitting makeshift curtains, while all along, two bedrooms upstairs had been vacant the whole time with comfy beds and curtains! Oh my!

I had to laugh! It's fascinating how things work out sometimes. Who knows? Without my annoying accommodation, I might have remained so comfortable that the old belief of unlovability might have stayed hidden, and that would have been a tragedy, preventing me from having one of the most important and powerful spiritual experiences of my entire life: being guided into the *Love* that, all along, lay in the heart of my belief of unlovability. What a gift. I am forever grateful to Gangaji, my mother ship. Thank you, thank you, thank you.

My relationship with stillness and silence hasn't always been an easy one. I used to be highly uncomfortable with silence. I constantly listened to music, mindlessly watched TV, or saw friends to avoid the silence. Back then, I regularly felt lonely when I wasn't with others. Although I didn't realize it at the time, I was distracting myself from my dark feelings, thoughts, and beliefs stemming from my childhood. And to boot, I numbed myself with alcohol and attention from guys because I wasn't ready to face the anguished, worthless, unlovable parts of me that lay inside.

In all honesty, it took me many years to fall in love with stillness and silence. I'm curious: What's your relationship with them like?

Many of us are terrified of opening the door to what lies deep in our psyche, believing the contents of our minds to be dark and sinister and best left hidden away. Perhaps we regard ourselves as damaged, nasty, selfish, or some other concoction of unbearable things. Overall, we'd much rather focus on making ourselves feel better than address our darkness within. As humans, we tend to avoid or run from what scares us.

My first experience of stillness came in my late twenties when I started attending yoga classes. During savasana, the teacher used guided imagery to promote relaxation. We breathed in calm energy as sparkly white air and expelled tension and stress as black or grey air. As we filled up with sparkly air, the darkness within gradually lightened until the exhaled air was as light as the incoming air. I felt like I was floating! It was so effective at promoting calm in me that it became a much-loved part of my kids' daily bedtime routine, fondly named "Fairy Dust."

During my Pilates teacher training in 2005, I discovered how focusing so intently on teeny-tiny muscles in my body created a welcome shift in my noisy, cluttered mind. I left the training sessions feeling serene and with a quiet mind. My troubles had vanished. Aside from introducing me to the benefits of mindfulness, my teachers taught me how to bring my attention inside my body, helping me notice bodily sensations more clearly. It was an immensely valuable tool because it also paved the way for me to become aware of my emotions.

Through Reiki, I became increasingly comfortable with stillness. It invokes profound stillness throughout my whole being. It always feels like such a blessed relief to experience this deep level of letting go.

Silence took on a new dimension when I participated in Brandon Bays's Journey™ Practitioner program. Some of the in-person training courses I attended involved considerable periods of silence. Aside from asking Brandon questions during class and the practice sessions with classmates, we had to remain in silence.

Being forbidden to chat with my friends was ridiculously hard for me. I genuinely struggled with it, especially at mealtimes when the urge to catch up with their news or tell a funny story became overwhelming. I confess that, occasionally, some whispering took place! I didn't manage to sink into the silence very far. I dipped in and out of it when it suited me.

Moving on to the world of silent blessings. Are you familiar with the term Darshan? I'd never heard of Darshan until a friend of mine, Kristen, mentioned that one was being held by Mother Meera in Boone, North Carolina. I didn't know who she was, so I looked her up and discovered that she is an Indian mystic, revered as a silent embodiment of the Divine Mother. She offers Darshan, silent blessings of *Love*, light, and Grace. In Hinduism,

Darshan means to see or be seen by a highly evolved being and receive a blessing.

I'm sure it won't surprise you to learn I was intrigued by her and keen to experience a silent blessing. I mean, how often do you get the chance to meet an *Avatar of Love?!* I couldn't pass it up! So, I drove to the majestic Blue Ridge Mountains.

Darshan took place in a hotel function room with around 300 attendees. In preparation for the blessing, we were given detailed instructions on what to do. With Mother Meera seated, when it was your turn, you knelt before her, bowing your head. Touching her tiny feet, clad in ankle-high, grey sports socks, was allowed if it called to you.

She placed her hands on your head, as she cleared obstructions in your body's energetic channels.

When she removed her hands, it was your cue to raise your head and look into her eyes as she transmitted light to you. Your Darshan was complete when she closed her eyes. Then, you returned to your seat, remaining in silent meditation until everyone had been blessed.

When it was my turn, and she placed her hands lightly on my head, I was surprised that I felt nothing other than the weight of her hands — no energetic sensations whatsoever. I raised my head and looked into her brown eyes. I'd expected to sense *Love* emanating from them. I didn't. As I gazed into her eyes, they seemed dark, expressionless, and empty, almost lifeless. Then, a strange thing happened; I felt compelled to close my eyes and they remained shut for several seconds. When my eyes decided to reopen, keen to continue the gaze, she immediately closed her eyes. My turn was done. "Next!"

I was so frustrated with myself for closing my eyes and missing most of the eye-gazing opportunity with Mother Meera. I felt cheated out of my Darshan. I wanted to ask for a do-over but thought better of it!

When I returned to my seat, I fell into a deep meditation. Later, I realized that, as an energetically sensitive person, I'd expected to have a profound spiritual experience in her presence. Yet, I'd sensed nothing energetically. I was baffled by what had taken place.

Curious to discover others' experiences, I struck up a conversation with a woman sitting next to me at breakfast the next morning. She was a delightful, interesting, and friendly person. She told me about powerful shifts she'd felt and said she'd seen and sensed *Love* blazing out of Mother Meera's eyes.

I still ponder about it sometimes. Perhaps Mother Meera showed me the void, pure consciousness, where we come from and return to when we die. The core of our being. Most likely, there is no need for my mind to understand what did or did not happen in Darshan that day.

By the time I attended my first in-person retreat with Gangaji in 2014, I was finally ready to embrace silence and stillness wholeheartedly. Leaving my expectations behind, I enjoyed being in silence and readily accepted her earnest invitation to dive deeply into my being. The energetic transmissions I received during my time with her created a gigantic shift inside me. I stopped looking to try and fix myself or heal myself. I accepted and forgave myself and key people in my life who I believed had hurt me. And I fell into an exquisite and profound experience of loving myself unconditionally. I came home to myself.

Her presence, which exudes *Love*, silence, and stillness, completely and utterly changed my life for the better.

If you want to experience Gangaji's offerings, there are plenty of her satsang videos on YouTube, and her website information is included in a resources page on my website. You'll find a link to that in the "Golden Nuggets" section at the back of the book.

Here are some final thoughts for you to consider before we move on to the next chapter about creativity.

The brilliant news is that you don't have to sit on a meditation cushion in a private place, with beautiful music playing in the background, to be able to tap into pure consciousness through silence and stillness. Sure, it's accessible there. But it's also readily available wherever you are: in the office, hiking, playing golf, surfing, at the grocery store, stuck in traffic, in the hospital, dropping off kids at school, or getting your nails done. You get the idea.

There is no need to spend money traveling to India, Bali, or other distant geographical locations to experience the power of silence. Wherever you are, it is constantly available to you, including at home, sitting on your comfy sofa, taking a moment to go inside. "Bingo!" There it is.

When we're willing to stop all mental activity, detach from our stories, regardless of where we are, and drop into our hearts with no expectations, we experience knowing ourselves as *Love*.

To our great surprise, we discover that *Love* is, in fact, "closer than your own breath," as Papaji — an Indian spiritual teacher of enlightenment — often shared.

Stillness and silence can be experienced in all emotions, from the most painful to the most delightful. In fact, all emotions are simply states that come and go, and those feelings arise and subside in silence and stillness.

So, if you're in the middle of a heated conversation or deep in excruciating grief at the death of a beloved, stillness and silence are right there, holding the space for all of it. All that is required is taking your attention inside, into your heart and breathing slowly, fully and deeply, letting go of your thoughts, and gently asking yourself to be shown what is untouched by these emotions. Be still, and stay out of your logical mind, as it will only tie itself in knots with this anyway, and surrender to the stillness. Then, wait and see what is revealed to you freshly in this moment.

When your mind is particularly restless, and you find it hard to settle and go inward, remember to experiment with shaking your body, or dancing, yoga, going for a brisk walk, or whatever else comes to mind. It may create an easier entry point to stillness for you.

As I mentioned earlier in the book, I often use effective tools to encourage my nervous system to relax. My favorites are tuning forks, singing bowls, crystals, and grounding tools. You'll find details about recommended suppliers in a resources page on my website. The link to that page can be found in the "Golden Nuggets" section later in the book. If you think you don't have time for stillness and silence, I lovingly encourage you to call yourself out on telling yourself stories of scarcity. Even five minutes of dipping into your inner world and welcoming what lies inside is massively beneficial for us.

Above all else, I nudge you to let go of seeing stillness and silence as something separate from you. In all honesty, it is your very nature, your essence, and it is always available when you drop inside.

You are an aspect of the Divine — a droplet of *Love*.

# 11

# AWAKENING OUR SENSUALITY AND LIFE-FORCE ENERGY

Are you extremely creative, or do you believe you don't have a creative bone in your body? Perhaps you regard yourself as not very creative compared to others. The truth is, we're all creative in our own unique ways.

Many of us were told when we were younger that we weren't very good at art or some other creative activity. Receiving that criticism often shuts down all or part of our creative flow. When I was around fifteen, my art teacher told me I lacked artistic talent. I felt embarrassed and deflated, and I believed that I wasn't any good compared to the excellent students in my class. That experience and the limiting beliefs it generated blocked my creativity for many years.

If we're not living a life imbued with creative juices, in some instances, a contributing factor may be that our parents, teachers, or peers played a role in steering us away from our creativity. Perhaps they encouraged us to focus on academic subjects rather than developing our artistic talents. They may have been concerned for our welfare, believing that we'd never be able to support ourselves financially if we went to art school. This isn't about blaming anyone for anything, merely understanding what might have affected our creative nature in the past.

The good news is that regardless of your relationship with creativity up to this moment, you can change it. If you wish, you can give yourself permission to be creative with a big dollop of childlike curiosity, wonder, and enthusiasm.

This chapter focuses on exploring ways to be creative, inspiring you to attempt things that call to you but daunt you — or perhaps picking up things that you loved as a child but, for one reason or another, cast aside.

Our creativity is our life-force energy in action. When the river of our life force flows strongly, it boosts our well-being, feeds our souls, and strengthens our self-love muscles — increasing our capacity to love ourselves unconditionally.

Opening up my creative pathways and letting my creativity run wild led to a powerful and intense awakening of my sensual, passionate nature and deepened my connection to the Divine. I discovered it's a fabulous way to express our feelings when life is tough. Creativity soothes and nourishes our souls and helps us transmute pain during difficult times. There is something so healing and enlivening about creating, whether planting a beautiful garden, getting artistic on canvas or paper, taking photos, writing a book, or making a delicious, colorful meal.

I've learned the hard way that it's crucial for me to give

my creative energy an ongoing outlet. When I suppress this energy, it feels intensely uncomfortable inside of me. Pressure builds up energetically in my inner world, and I'm more irritable, argumentative, impatient, and frustrated. I also feel a degree of disconnection from my spiritual guides and the Divine when I'm blocking the flow.

Take a moment to remember what you loved to do creatively as a child that you haven't done in a long while. Also, what would you love to have a go at but keep putting off or continually talk yourself out of doing? Sculpture, pottery, poetry, writing a screenplay, photography, crochet, planting wildflowers? What's calling to you? What tickles your fancy?

Perhaps you're coming up with reasons why you can't do it. You know, the old favorites: *I'm no good at it; I'm not creative; I don't know how to go about that; I'd love to, but I haven't got the time;* or maybe, *People will laugh at me.*

Other obstacles that can prevent us from being creative are perfectionist tendencies, unrealistic expectations, putting pressure on ourselves, taking it all too seriously, and focusing on the outcome rather than the creative process. All of these can stifle our creativity. Thankfully, there are effective ways to clear unhelpful beliefs, freeing us to jump into the creative flow. I regularly use EFT, The Work, and ACT tools to clear out any troublesome or persistent beliefs. All of them are highly effective and make a massive difference.

And do bear in mind that nobody on this Earth needs to see your creative output. Unless you want them to, of course. It doesn't need to be what anyone else might describe as "amazing." The healing part of creativity is all about the process rather than the result. So, I urge you to be playful, do what you genuinely enjoy, and be curious to see what emerges without judgment.

Be honest with yourself; what's your relationship like with your creative nature?

I've discovered that I'm wildly passionate about creating and sharing beauty with the world and encouraging others to do the same. Bringing something gorgeous into form from a blank canvas or a patch of soil feels delightful and touches my soul in deeply pleasurable ways.

All in all, I reckon if a creative idea lights you up in some way, even a fraction, it's worth playing around with.

What follows are some of the ways that I love to be creative. They may inspire or remind you of things you have long forgotten. As you read my words, notice what ideas come to you for your own creative adventures.

As a young girl, I loved making things. Perhaps it was triggered by school sewing projects. Back then, where I grew up, girls had to take sewing and home economics classes. I adored embroidering things. And I learned how to knit, creating long, itchy scarves or squares for plant pots to sit on. As a teenager, I made some clothing items, and in my adult years, I created fancy cushion covers, blinds, and curtains. When I was pregnant with my daughter, I spent the last few weeks before she was due to arrive knitting jumpers for her. Wool garments on newborns? What was I thinking?! Still, it kept me busy, and the complicated patterns were a wonderful challenge for my mind.

I was brought up by very musical parents and as a child, I played several musical instruments: recorder, piano, clarinet, flute, and cornet. It came naturally to me. I read music with ease and took my musical ability for granted. Practicing was painfully dull, but I enjoyed playing in school orchestras.

I fondly remember enthusiastically blasting out festive carols at my grandparents' farmhouse during Christmas Day family gatherings. I was part of a family brass trio: my dad on the baritone horn, my brother on the slide trombone, and me on the cornet.

These days I love singing, mainly while driving, writing, painting, and dancing. It's so fun belting out all the words to Human League's "Dare" album or murdering Kate Bush's "Wuthering Heights." My word, Kate, that's a tricky one and way outside of my alto range, but it never stops me from singing it with gusto!

In 2023, James bought me a RAV Vast handpan in the scale of Celtic B minor. This steel percussion instrument produces deep, soothing vibrations, and we'd fallen in love with its sound during a healing session in Santa Fe earlier that year. We were keen to learn to play it. I love the freedom of learning to play this gorgeous instrument without putting any pressure on myself to be good at it. It's a meditative and calming practice that relaxes my nervous system as the soulful vibrations flow through my body.

Do you love to dance? I do! I derive so much pleasure

from dancing. As a young girl, I was a keen ballet and tap dancer. I spent hours practicing my tap routines on the concrete path by the back door to the kitchen, leaving little white marks of joy as I tapped away. I adored performing in our dance company's shows at the Royal Hall in Harrogate, wearing sparkly costumes my mum had spent hours sewing for me.

My enthusiasm was dampened when my dance instructors remarked that I was too tall to be a ballet dancer. I completely lost interest after that. That was the end of dance classes for me. But my love of dance continued to thrive. As a teenager, I danced endlessly at discos and nightclubs. I stayed on the dance floor for so long that friends took shifts dancing with me! Feeling the rhythm and moving my body in response to the music lit me up, and pure joy coursed through every level of my being.

Although my disco and clubbing days are over, I dance around my house these days, especially when no one else is home! My soul is delighted when I dance. Even when I exhaust myself, the smile in my heart, the sparkle in my eyes, and my exuberant energy refuel and nourish me beyond words.

"My brush always gives a tremor of pleasure when I let it paint a flower," remarked English artist Winifred Nicholson.

Few things elicit as much delight for me as mixing colors and slapping on and scraping off oil paints, over and over, until my interpretation of a bunch of flowers emerges from the canvas. My intention is to consistently capture the essence of the flowers and convey their energy and beauty as best as I can.

I'd dabbled with art as a child, loving art projects at school and enthusiastically creating pictures of scenes around my grandparents' farm using pastels. As I mentioned earlier, at secondary school, my art teachers were unimpressed by my efforts and dismissed me as a terrible artist, which led to my rejecting my artistic side for many years.

But in my early twenties, something deep inside me whispered in my ear, nudging me to return to painting. So, I signed up for a night class to learn the art of watercolor painting. I'll be honest: there wasn't much flow or fun back then. I was determined to make my painting look exactly like my subject and was horribly critical of myself when it didn't come up to scratch in my eyes. It brought out the harsh perfectionist in me.

Watercolors were a deeply frustrating and stressful medium for me back then. My work rarely matched up to my high expectations. And as watercolor painting is unforgiving, I knew the game was over when I messed up a piece because there was no chance of improving it. So, I'd screw up the paper and toss it in the bin in a disappointed and self-sabotaging flurry.

In my thirties, my kids attended art classes with a local artist. I loved seeing their artwork and reveled in how much they loved creating. I began to dream about painting again, but I held myself back because I feared being useless.

My artistic stirrings remained dormant until we emigrated to the USA, and I was living in Madison, New Jersey.

I've shared in an earlier chapter how I had a horrendous time during those early years of living in America. It was a struggle to integrate into American culture, and I was desperately grieving my homeland.

I was thrown into numerous, intense dark nights of the soul, and my life was in turmoil. I was miserable, lonely, isolated, feeling rejected and abandoned, and far away from my British support network. I'd begun healing my childhood wounds in earnest, and it was seriously tough going for a while.

In the middle of my struggles, feeling lost at sea, I felt guided to sign up for an adult education class on acrylic painting. That small action changed the trajectory of my life. Diving into painting at one of my lowest points ended up being the very thing that awoke my femininity, sensuality, and passionate nature.

During those years in New Jersey, painting became an incredibly healing activity for me. As I mixed colors and brushed them onto my canvases, massive waves of emotion arose, flooding my body and making it hard to continue painting in that moment. It became so overwhelming at times that I had to escape to the bathroom to let the tears flow in privacy. I felt out of control, and it was scary at times. I didn't realize it at the time, but a deep purge of my past was taking place, and I began awakening to my true nature.

Little by little, I was releasing complex and painful wounds from my childhood that had been triggered by feeling stranded high and dry in suburban New Jersey.

With all of this going on, I did my very best to look after my family while keeping to myself the enormity of what was happening. I learned to wear invisible masks, attempting to show the world that I was doing just fine. But the truth was, inside, I was falling to pieces, disintegrating. I now realize it was a necessary part of my evolution, preparing me for a rebirth.

A couple of years later, James suggested that I take up oil painting. I loved the idea of being able to paint on a much bigger scale. The nature of oil paints would open up that world to me, and I adored their luminous quality. James found a local teacher with great reviews named Andy Braitman, and I felt the nudge to sign up for lessons.

My years at the Braitman Studio in Charlotte were an exhilarating rollercoaster of a ride. Andy is an exceptionally talented and successful artist. He's also a superb teacher who generously shares his knowledge and expertise with his students and is very entertaining in the process. A big character, for sure!

He blew up my existing painting style. In the early months of painting at his studio, my bruised and battered ego often felt distressed and demoralized. But I kept showing up throughout the destructive process, striving to dig deeper for the gold I knew lay within. For a short while, I genuinely believed I'd never be able to paint well again!

Then, the magic began to happen. Gradually, something started to rise out of the ashes. Everything Andy had been teaching me — about color theory, composition, values, brush strokes, application methods, and so much more — started to fall into place.

Andy talked incessantly, but beyond what he taught us through his words, something profound was transmitted to me as I witnessed him deep in his creative flow as he painted during demos. The energy, enthusiasm, and passion were palpable. To date, I've never seen so much passion contained within one person! It was infectious and an immensely precious gift in my life.

Andy pushed me way beyond my comfort zone. It required me to trust him and trust the process that was unfolding. That wasn't always easy for me, and I sometimes wondered if he was completely bonkers.

However, an incredible transformation took place over those years, and when I moved to Connecticut in 2017, I left his studio as a confident and capable artist.

In addition to improving my artistic abilities, something else was happening, too.

Through the dismantling of the old ways and the formation of the new, I became aware of how much I'd been suppressing the creative, feminine, sensual, and passionate parts of me. I'd been trying to manipulate how these important aspects of me were permitted to show up in my life. I'd pretty much locked them in the dingy basement.

I'd spent years trying to diminish them because they felt uncontrollably powerful. I feared that if I gave them free rein, they might destroy me and the comfortable, safe life I had created for myself. As far as sensible Rachel was concerned, those intense, passionate energies had led me astray many times. So, I regarded them as unwelcome, delinquent, wild, and untrustworthy. Basically, I'd tamed myself, believing that the real me was socially unacceptable, and I was terrified of the consequences of letting loose. In my younger years, I'd often been burned when others told me, "You're too intense" or "You're too much." In response, I'd dimmed my light, believing that I was the one who had to change to be accepted by others.

During those years of painting with Andy, I began to unveil my sensual, passionate, feminine sides. Those wonderful, ecstatic parts of me were set free, and I fell into embracing and loving all of who I am.

As the process continued to unfold, I became less inhibited and more courageous, and I felt the flow of life in the most incredible ways — orgasmic on every level, going far beyond the sexual, with energy coursing through all my energy centers, a whole new way of existing. I was in uncharted territory, with every cell of my being vibrating and tingling in delicious harmony — consciousness aware of itself in human form.

I'm forever grateful to Andy for his sense of humor, patience, encouragement, and belief in me and for generously sharing his knowledge and incredible talent with me.

Along the artistic path, I discovered that muses in human form are at best unreliable. They tend to turn to dust in your hands, leaving us feeling high and dry. I realized it's often a way in which many of us give our creative power away to others.

The more I painted and the deeper I went into my own heart through various spiritual practices, the clearer I saw that the Divine is my only muse. Anything or anyone else is a pitiful substitute. In this realization, I came home to myself with love, compassion, and understanding.

I still love to paint. As I sit at my desk in my art studio, writing this to you, now and then I gaze at my artwork surrounding me. Part of me is writing this book, and yet, at the same time, part of me is preparing to finish two big canvases. They are beginning to call to me, and I'm excited about returning to them and giving them my full attention. Just as soon as the first draft of this book is finished, they will be gleaming with wet paint.

Some of my favorite things to paint are energies, water, landscapes, and flowers. I have an ongoing love affair with flowers, especially roses, as they have the highest vibration of all blooms, and I adore their scent and form. It's an ongoing process of getting out of my critical mind and into the creative flow, surrendering control, and letting energy move freely so I can capture their divine essence as loosely as possible.

I doubt I will ever tire of the incredible satisfaction and fulfillment that making art brings. Passion and life-force energy pump through my veins as I slap on and scrape off the oil paint.

My love affair with flowers led me to create gorgeous gardens resplendent with colorful blooms, diverse textures, shapes, and an interesting array of foliage colors.

Listening to tall grasses blow in the breeze is one of the most deeply relaxing and calming sounds I know. Every spring, I get such a thrill watching the perennial plants and bulbs emerge from the soil to greet the fresh, expectant air.

As a young mum in the UK, I taught myself all about gardening. I read tons of books and avidly watched the BBC's *Gardeners' World* on a Friday night, making notes on the horticultural jobs for that weekend. It brought me so much joy choosing plants, preparing the beds, planting out my purchases, and bringing the design to life. I loved pruning and other gardening jobs that garden maintenance involves. It feels so good to be outside, working in the garden, feeling soil underneath your fingernails, and noticing all the delightful changes through the seasons.

I've created colorful, beautiful, serene gardens in every house I've owned over the last twenty-five years. That process takes a lot of time and energy, so I'm looking forward to the day I inherit a fabulous garden from a previous owner!

Like painting, gardening is another way I love to create and share beauty with the world. In fact, I often blend the two and paint my garden in bloom, in all of its glory.

Over the years, I've received many compliments on my gardens. People walking their dogs have remarked on how much they love my tulip and daffodil displays and how their colors and vibrancy bring them so much joy in early spring. Others have said how they love that my garden has something interesting to enjoy in every season of the year. Instead of erecting a high, solid privacy fence to block the view of my back garden, I installed a stylish black metal fence that enables passers-by to enjoy the splendor.

This beauty is meant to be shared. As we gaze and appreciate it, we are reminded of our inner beauty. Enough said.

In some ways, it's still a surprise to me that I'm writing this book, mainly because I've never thought of myself as a writer.

In my mind, my daughter Jess is the writer in my family. She excels at it and writes for a living in the world of advertising. The words have always seemed to flow so naturally and effortlessly through her onto the page.

Labels are strange things. What have you called yourself? My list of labels includes daughter, sister, friend, bridesmaid, wife, mother, aunt, hydrologist, business development executive, Pilates instructor, Reiki master, NLP trainer, transformational coach, spiritual guide, and artist. In truth, none of them define who we are; we are so much more than our labels, but as human beings, labels are useful as a way of categorizing and simplifying the world.

About fourteen years ago, while I was undertaking a private Akashic Records mentorship with Brynne Dippell, I received messages that I would write three books. In case you're unfamiliar with the term, the Akashic Records are best described as an energetic library that holds the story of every soul's journey — past, present, and future. When we access the records, insightful information is shared with us through the Akashic Masters, Teachers, and Loved Ones.

My Akashic team reassured me that the information for my first book was ready and waiting to be downloaded through me from the Akashic realm. They shared that all I had to do was reach up above my head, get myself out of the way, and let it flow through me. Well, I repeatedly tried to connect with it. It was deeply frustrating because I received fragments of downloads, but it wasn't flowing easily. Self-doubt was more prevalent than the act of writing. So, after a while, I put it aside. I felt rather puzzled and deflated. It seemed to me that, for whatever reason, I just wasn't ready.

I now realize that other experiences needed to happen in my life for me to be truly ready to write this book. I also needed to clear out fears about vulnerability that were holding me back from sharing myself with the world in this bold way.

The death of my dad in 2022, although a tragic and sad event, was also an incredible gift. It created an unstoppable momentum in me that centered around getting serious about writing this book.

To gain confidence, I completed a couple of book-writing courses before signing up with The Self Publishing Agency (TSPA) to publish my forthcoming book.

I was ready. It was time to birth *Droplets of Love.*

While I'm not keen on labels, after all these months of sharing my heart on the page with you, I now regard myself as a writer. And I'm very proud of myself, especially for my determination, enthusiasm, and willingness to share so much of myself with you. It is done with the sole intention that you might benefit in some shape or form by reading it.

I received an invaluable gift from Gangaji, a transmission of *Love* that guided me to the core of my being, where stillness and *Love* reside. Writing this book is my tender and authentic way of passing that torch of realization to you.

Creativity is an essential component in looking after ourselves mentally, emotionally, physically, and spiritually. It expands our capacity to love and accept ourselves just as we are. Creativity is far too important to be brushed aside and treated as an indulgence.

Interestingly, results from numerous scientific studies indicate that when we engage in creative activities, anxiety can diminish or even disappear. Even scribbling on a piece of paper can have this calming effect. So, the next time anxiety floods your being, get creative!

I sincerely hope my words on creativity have re-ignited a creative flame inside of you or encouraged you to explore a new creative outlet.

Please give yourself the freedom to go with the flow of your creative interests. They may evolve over time. What you enjoyed as a child may be a springboard into a new idea that speaks to you now.

Be curious, be playful, and most of all, be willing to focus on the creative process rather than the outcome.

Give yourself permission to be all of who you are. Along the way, you may discover that aspects of your magnificence you've suppressed in the past re-emerge as you let your creativity run wild.

Take a leap of faith by embracing and owning your creative birthright. Always remember, I'm right here, cheering you on and inspiring you to take the plunge.

# 12

# CONNECTION BREEDS HARMONY

Something profoundly moving happened in 2024 that I'd love to share with you. It reminded me why I'm so passionate about guiding people to the stillness inside of them, where they can rest, and love and nourish themselves.

Passionate about authentic, soulful communities, I created a monthly online gathering called "Self-Love Sanctuary." It was a welcoming, safe, sacred space where people could experience themselves as *Love* and clear away obstacles that were veiling their connection to their intuition and divinity.

At the beginning of one of these soulful gatherings, a participant, Shirley, a delightful woman in her eighties, shared that she'd never had an experience of self-love. She didn't know what it was or how it would feel.

We talked for a while, and then I led the participants into a gentle, loving, guided meditation. My words took them into the core of their beings. They were guided into their hearts and experienced pure acceptance, reassurance, and support from the powerful force of *Love* that resides inside each and every one of us.

I checked in with everyone after the meditation. It turned out that Shirley had dipped into the *Love* that lay at her core for the first time in her life.

With a slightly confused look on her face, as if her mind couldn't comprehend what had just happened, and with a glint in her eye combined with a look of wonder, she shared what had taken place during the meditation. On journeying into her heart, she had discovered a bright light. It appeared as a blue light sparkling like diamonds. She also shared that she'd found a ledge inside her heart where she knew she could go and sit whenever she wanted to, soaking in the loving, gentle energy. Shirley sensed that this energy is always available to her, and to experience it, she just needs to turn inwards and enter her heart space.

What an extraordinary gift for Shirley. It demonstrates so perfectly that we can experience this divine connection at any stage in our lives. It's never too late to join the party! I'm deeply grateful that I witnessed her authentic realization of who she truly is. Shirley's experience is one of many beautiful moments etched into my heart.

Our connection to our true selves as aspects of *Love* is the most important connection in our human existence. When we experience that force of *Love*, even if only for a few seconds, it can utterly change our lives.

This ever-present energy of *Love* is ready and waiting to support and guide us with everything going on in our lives. However, it doesn't necessarily mean that we'll always get what we want, but I believe we are brought the experiences and insights we most need to assist our soul's evolution. *Love* certainly seems to smooth the way and make difficult events more bearable. All that is required is to drop into our hearts, direct our awareness to the expansive, loving energy and invite it into our everyday lives.

Our relationship with this inner lover deepens exponentially when we make time for it regularly, meet it with our full, loving attention, and bow to it. What a glorious feeling it is when we bask in the vibration of unconditional, all-encompassing *Love*.

In my view, the journey through each lifetime presents us with countless opportunities to surrender to *Love* — releasing our futile attempts to control our reality and ultimately letting *Love* take the lead. I know from personal experience, that is no small undertaking. It requires tremendous trust and courage, but the rewards are well worth it.

Sharing my story about Shirley demonstrates how valuable it is to connect to the Divine and how simple it can be to do so. The energy of *Love* exists at our core, and that *Love* is an aspect of the Divine. When we tap into that energy of *Love*, the potential exists for us to heal and transform.

In the early years of my healing journey, my exceptionally overactive, analytical mind often interfered when I tried to connect with the Divine. It wasn't until I spoke with Gangaji during a residential retreat in 2014, that I received an undeniable, strong taste of this *Love* inside. Quite simply, it stopped me in my tracks. What I discovered is that my ego had been desperately trying to access the Divine within, using all kinds of tools and techniques.

Oh, how the Universe has a sense of humor! What I realized is that when I stopped trying so hard to connect to the Divine and instead, remained still, as if by magic, there it was, right there: *Love*. Pure consciousness. So close that I was continually overlooking it.

Please bear in mind that sometimes it can take a while for us to be ready to put down all the "doing" and give ourselves permission to be totally still. Being patient and letting go of expectations can work wonders.

When we chase after *Love*, making it into an object, it's nowhere to be seen. It's elusive, constantly outrunning us.

I needed a nudge from a spiritual teacher to discover the Divine inside of me. That doesn't mean the same is true for you. You may find that you can make this discovery without a teacher.

When you dive deeply into spirituality, it's easy to find yourself floating around in the ethers. We can feel disconnected from our human selves, with spiritual platitudes swirling around. I struggled with this for a few years. Regularly spending hours meditating each day, I often felt directionless and lacked momentum. I realized I needed assistance with blending spiritual teachings with regular life.

Tosha Silver, another spiritual teacher I highly recommend, has a delightful and practical way of putting spiritual teachings into the relatable context of our everyday human lives. Her courses have played an important role in helping me to bridge the gap between spiritual concepts (which can be ethereal, abstract, and dissociated) and our humanness, which can be messy and far from perfect.

Feeling connected in some way is a fundamental need for most people.

It's important to realize that connection means different things to each of us. You may or may not resonate with what matters most to me about connection.

What does the word "connection" conjure up in you? Which aspects of connection are most important to you?

My most valued connections are these: all aspects of myself, my family, the Divine, the Akashic Records, my spirit guides, my friends, my soul tribe, people in the afterlife, community, and nature.

Through a couple of private mentorships with different teachers, I learned how to access the Akashic Records. If you recall from the previous chapter, the Records are best described as an energetic archive of our souls' past, present, and future possibilities. The energy within the Records is always loving, calming, and healing.

I treasure my connection with the Akashic Records and tap into them most days to assist myself or my clients. They are an incredibly valuable resource when we seek to understand the dynamics at play with specific relationships, circumstances, and events in our lives. Accessing the Akashic Records can be tremendously healing and beneficial, helping us navigate the ups and downs of human existence.

Many years ago, I began to receive guidance from a collection of beings who called themselves the Sisterhood of Navarham. I regard them as an aspect of my Higher Self.

They channel powerful healing meditations and play an important role in guiding me when working with clients and holding gatherings. They are always there to offer me support, insights, and comfort. Unconditional *Love* abounds in their presence.

As my relationships with the Divine, the Akashic Records, and the Sisterhood of Navarham deepened, I stopped feeling lonely. That was a blessed relief. The desperate need to be with others vanished, and I morphed into being extremely happy and content in my own company.

We can all learn how to tap into the Akashic Records and channel aspects of our Higher Selves. Connecting with them gives us an ever-present supply of *Love*, wisdom, and support.

Our inner wisdom tends to flow more freely when we breathe deeply, quieten our mind, come into our heart space, and ask for guidance. This connection to our intuition strengthens when we trust what we sense and act on what we receive.

Oracle Cards can be a helpful way to deepen our relationship with our Higher Self. If they are a new concept to you: they are a spiritual deck of cards, offering gentle guidance, insights, or a daily nudge from the Universe. Whether you're seeking clarity on a specific issue or just looking for a bit of inspiration, they help you tap into your inner wisdom and connect with your Higher Self.

Although Oracle Cards are a valuable tool, I encourage you to always use discernment with the information you receive. Always check in with your body, your inner knowing, to see if the guidance resonates before taking any action.

Our bodies are an incredibly powerful navigation tool because they always tell us what is true for us.

Here's a quick reminder on how to check in. It works for Oracle Cards, messages from guides or the Divine, and everything in the human realm.

When you want to determine if something resonates, notice how your body responds in terms of sensations as you receive or read the guidance. That will illuminate your true answer.

Unpleasant or negative responses will have their own set of characteristics. Tightness, tension, pain, or restriction may be felt. Pleasurable or positive responses will be shown through a different set of sensations. Feeling expansive, open, warm, or tingly are common indicators.

Becoming familiar with our body's unique signals and tuning in regularly to see how our body is responding makes navigating our lives infinitely smoother.

I use my inner guidance daily as I make small decisions, like which bike route to take, which crystal to meditate with, or which herbal tea to drink, as well as much larger ones. I have used it to determine which town to move to and which house to buy.

In addition to tuning into our body's sensations, it's also important to become aware of our thoughts and feelings at any given time. Doing so helps us to build more loving and compassionate relationships with ourselves.

Are you telling yourself painful, repetitive thoughts?

Are there emotions you've been ignoring or trying to bury? Are there inner youngsters feeling unloved or unheard, calling for your attention?

When we are aware of our feelings and thoughts, an opportunity arises to welcome it all, to embrace the energy of what we discover while detaching from the narrative.

Developing loving, compassionate, and understanding relationships with our inner children is essential in helping us to heal from painful events. Once we care for ourselves in this way and create a nonjudgmental space for the parts that don't feel good, their power is greatly diminished, mainly because those aspects of us usually crave being seen, heard, and met. When we stop asking others to feed these inner desires and longings, and instead show up fully for ourselves, lasting transformations and healings occur.

Whether you engage in this profound inner work independently or with the support of a practitioner, the key is to approach it with tenderness, compassion and openness.

Feeling connected to a soul tribe can be enormously valuable, healing, inspiring, and comforting. My definition of a soul tribe is the people with whom we have soulful, authentic, loving relationships. We resonate with them and feel a deep bond with them. They may include friends, family members, practitioners, and people we encounter for an instant.

Have you ever met someone with whom, the moment you laid eyes on them, you sensed a deep familiarity, as though you'd known them forever? When we experience that phenomenon, they are often part of our soul tribe — kindred spirits with whom we shared previous lifetimes.

It might sound good, but their presence in our lives isn't always wonderful. Despite the close bond and familiarity, those relationships can sometimes be outrageously painful, creating excruciating experiences for us. Our lives can be turned upside down and inside out. However, on a soul level, where only *Love* exists between us, we arranged these interactions before birth to help each other learn valuable soul lessons and evolve.

In the early years of my healing journey, I yearned for deep, close friendships with spiritual people. And plenty of those friendships materialized.

Rather than giving these friendships space to evolve naturally, I had an idealized view of what spiritual friendships should be like: meditating together, learning from each other, holding space for each other, and helping each other grow and evolve spiritually. In some cases, my fantasy prevented me from showing up authentically. I often reined myself in and censored my truth.

Being spiritual isn't about playing the role of how we think spiritual people should behave. Rather than conforming to a spiritual stereotype, being spiritual is about embracing all of who we are, and accepting and meeting every aspect. Spirituality isn't about bypassing the tough emotions like anger. Getting angry now and then is part of being a human! Dive into its energy field. Let it flow through you. Give yourself permission to be the authentic you, just as you are.

There can be a tendency for spiritual people to live their lives rather separately from others, regarding themselves as special in some way. They can become dissociated from the reality of our messy human existence and be unable to show up in meaningful, supportive ways for those moving through traumatic events.

In my thirties, I transitioned from being completely disinterested in spirituality to becoming a deeply spiritual person.

It's uncomfortable admitting this now, but I used to regard myself as a special spiritual being. I distanced myself from several friends who weren't spiritual and did an excellent job of hanging out in lofty spiritual realms.

If you're experiencing that or have in the past, go easy on yourself. Many of us on a spiritual journey go through that phase. Usually, a point is reached where we can't tolerate the ongoing delusion for another second, and we find ourselves ready to meet our spiritual ego in compassionate, honest, and humble ways. It's a necessary part of our evolution.

Hard jolts in life, like serious health issues, divorce, losing a job, or the death of a beloved, can pop that spiritual bubble. Life gets gritty, difficult, and traumatic sometimes.

We are all eternal beings and aspects of *Love*, and at the same time, we are also having a human existence in a physical body. We are both energetic beings and human beings intertwined. Whether we regard ourselves as spiritual or not, everyone is a blend of the two.

Those spiritual friendships didn't give me what I yearned for. The truth is no one can give us what we long for at our core. The longing we experience is the call to come home to ourselves as aspects of the Divine.

These days, I adore being around interesting, bright, creative, loving, open-hearted, humorous people. I still enjoy the company of spiritual folk, but only those who are reasonably well-grounded and don't take themselves too seriously.

As we heal from our troubles and traumas, we raise our vibration. In doing so, we discover that we fall out of resonance with some people and into resonance with others. It's to be expected. As we change, some friendships will end, and new ones will emerge.

It can be tough to let go of friends. We may hold on tightly to them even though the friendship no longer feels good.

I love the analogy of a friend being like a bird sitting on our open palm, free to fly away whenever they wish, with nothing holding them captive. Both parties have free will to go in different directions. Ultimately, this approach feels so much better than resisting change by maintaining a death grip on the bird!

I'm incredibly grateful for all the friends in my life, past and present. I love them all dearly.

❋

I'm guided by how it feels energetically to be around people. I spend time with those I enjoy being with and limit my contact with those who drain me.

It's wise to be very discerning about who we spend our time with, especially if we're energetically sensitive. When I get "taken out" by a depleting encounter, it can take days to get back into harmonious flow.

Think of who you spend time with. How do you feel when you are with them? How do you feel after your interactions? Be honest with yourself. Are you spending time with people you don't feel good with or don't trust?

I've sifted out some friendships that weren't healthy for me. One of those was a friend who used to dig and poke around until she found something that wasn't going well in my life, which seemed to give her energy and please her.

Is there anyone like that in your friend circle?

She'd had some rough knocks in life, and I'd done my best to support her. But after several years, I got fed up with her pattern of making herself feel better by trying to make me feel bad.

I decided to make a change and started prioritizing my needs by enforcing healthy boundaries and giving the friendship a wide berth.

Being discerning about our friendships and making wise decisions about our allocation of time and energy are essential parts of loving ourselves.

Do you find yourself saying "yes" to invitations without checking if it's in alignment with your deeper self?

I love going out with friends and having fun. It can be like trying to stop stampeding wild horses when an invite comes my way. Most often, I want to say "YES!" But even with those I love spending time with, sometimes it isn't beneficial for me to go out.

It can be hard to slow down sufficiently to check in with our deeper selves before replying to an invite. For most of us, declining invitations can be very awkward. Mind you, it's often easier to make a good decision in the first place rather than rashly accepting and then having to backtrack later.

Feeling connected to family is important to many of us, giving us a sense of belonging. I adore my family.

My close bonds with James, Jess, and Josh are extraordinarily important to me. We're a tight-knit clan. They are always in my heart and soul. I'm so grateful for their love, support, and presence in my life and feel extremely fortunate.

As you've read, some relationships with my family of origin have been very challenging. I've healed a multitude of childhood wounds, and I've forgiven both of my parents completely and utterly. I honestly believe that they did the best they could in the circumstances.

I love spending time with my mum. Twice a year, I pop over the Atlantic to visit her. I have a lot of laughs with her. She has a great sense of humor, can be very entertaining, and is a loyal and caring person.

Wanting to make the most of our time together, I've learned to head off her pattern of disaster thinking and obsessive, critical thoughts. I've stopped trying to change her, and I've come to accept her just as she is. I realize it was arrogant of me to believe she needed to change. It turns out that I was the one who needed to shift my behavior.

Changing how I respond when things get sticky between us has improved our relationship immeasurably. I give myself time-outs and focus on the positive elements of our mother-daughter relationship. And I'm very grateful that she's in my life in such a lovely way.

Humans are social beings and are instinctively hard-wired to belong to communities, desiring close bonds with others.

However, these days, many of us feel an acute loss of community and, to varying degrees, feel disconnected from others. Perhaps in part, the dominance of TV and the internet, the ever-increasing pace of life, and geographically dispersed families have encouraged that sense of distance and dissociation. Feeling busy and perpetually short of time can leave us feeling stressed and isolated from others.

I have a question for you that is dear to my heart. How can we help to turn the tide by contributing towards creating authentic, compassionate, harmonious, loving communities?

Plenty of opportunities exist to play a role in building desirable communities. Here are a few ideas to whet your appetite.

As we heal our emotional and mental wounds from the past, we raise our vibration. In doing so, we become a valuable, much-needed gift to the world. Then we can show up, simply being ourselves and allowing our radiance to be shared with those we meet. This radiance is, in fact, the energy of the Divine being channeled through us. Remembering that moves our ego aside, keeps us humble, and ensures we are of greatest service to others.

Looking into people's eyes and smiling acts like a magic balm. Asking people how they are, listening deeply to the answer, and being fully present with them is one of the greatest gifts that we can offer to another. When done authentically and genuinely, it has a healing effect and gives us both a tremendous boost. It can contribute towards neutralizing dense emotions like fear, overwhelm, doubt, mistrust, and anger that are prevalent in our society.

When we witness someone having an outburst in a store, rather than taking on their anger or judging them, we can take some deep breaths and send them light and blessings instead. I often visualize popping a love bomb, akin to a calming, soothing bath bomb, into the crown of their head. No words are needed.

With an intention to create and foster loving communities, even the tiniest of actions make a tremendous difference to the whole. Never underestimate that.

Whether we let cars out into the flow of traffic, open a

door for someone, or have a friendly chat with a sales associate, it all contributes to creating a richer, more harmonious life for humanity.

While I don't regard myself as a medium, I do seem to have an ability to connect with dead people sometimes. I have no idea how open you are to encounters with loved ones who have transitioned. Whatever your beliefs are, I invite you to keep an open mind as you read on.

I'm going to share a few spirit experiences with you because they facilitated healing and connections with the powerful force of *Love*.

In 2005, I had an encounter with a dear relative who had died. It happened during Reiki training in the UK. On the first day, the teacher relayed to me that a man in spirit form was here to see me. Trust me when I say this: at that point in my life, I was totally shut down to the possibility of ghosts and had zero interest in it.

To be honest, when he mentioned what he was sensing, I was nervous and scared, but at the same time, part of me was curious.

As I relaxed and opened my awareness, I felt the energetic presence of my beloved Grandad Eric, my mother's father. He had been a Lancashire hill farmer. He was a tough, courageous, good man with a colorful character and a superb sense of humor. He had been one of the shining lights in my turbulent younger years, and I loved him dearly.

He died in his eighties when I was about thirty-one years old. I'd heard that he was fading fast, but to my intense sadness and frustration, I was struck down with a nasty virus when I received the news. So, unfortunately, I didn't get to say goodbye before he died.

I was distraught that I hadn't been able to see him in the last few days of his life. I didn't get closure. I didn't get to say "I love you" or thank him for everything he'd done for me.

Back in the Reiki training room, I sensed his energy. It truly felt like him. I have no better way of describing it than that. Unfamiliar sensations flooded my body. I felt strong, disconcerting surges of pulsing energy. Every cell in my body was buzzing intensely. It was an extremely pleasurable sensation, akin to receiving the biggest, most loving hug imaginable. It felt so good. I was saturated with *Love*.

Realizing I could speak with him, I told him I was incredibly sorry that I'd been too sick to see him to say goodbye. I told him I loved him and how grateful I was to him for being such a wonderful person in my life — a force of positivity, support, and laughter in my childhood.

To my amazement, I heard him reply. He said he understood why I couldn't make it. He said he loved me too, that it was all okay, and it was time for me to let go of being upset about what happened. He reassured me that now we'd made the connection, I could call him in whenever I wanted to. An almighty sense of peace and *Love* coursed through my veins.

I have no idea how long this experience lasted; it might have been less than a minute, but it felt like a very long time.

Going into that Reiki training, I had no clue I would receive loving and tender closure from Grandad Eric. Connecting with him enabled me to heal and move on from the upsetting circumstances of his death.

Since then, I've connected with other people in spirit. Some have arrived at difficult, stressful, worrying times. Two dear soul sisters, Kit and Susan, who both died of cancer a few years ago, showed up when I was called back for further screening after a mammogram showed something suspicious. As I sat in the examination room, waiting for the doctor to come in and speak to me, I felt their loving, kind, supportive energy right there with me. I felt their energies in my heart, and they were embracing me. They soothed me and encouraged me to breathe deeply and stay calm. It was such a gift to sense their presence when I most needed support and reassurance.

Then, there were the times when spirits showed up for the benefit of others. Many years ago, I was working with a mother whose adult son had taken his own life. We were in the middle of a Reiki session when I sensed that his energy was in the room with us, and it began swirling around in a vortex above her body. I sensed it entering her chest, right into her heart. She was a devout Catholic, so being careful not to freak her out, I shared that he was in her heart, and she could connect with him whenever she wanted to. It was such an amazing, energetic experience that I felt honored to witness. She received a beautiful heart healing that day. After the session, she shared that she felt noticeably lighter and told me that she'd sensed her son in the room, which had brought her tremendous comfort.

What's your relationship like with nature? Many of us have become highly disconnected from the natural world, spending most of our time indoors or driving.

Connecting with the natural world in its array of glorious forms is incredibly healing and good for our souls. Nature is an exquisite catalyst for slowing down our busy, chaotic minds. Tuning into the rhythm of life and the heartbeat of Mother Nature boosts our overall well-being and encourages healing by reducing stress and overwhelm.

Do you love the smell of rain? Do you delight in the feeling of sand or lush grass underneath your naked feet? Do you adore swimming in lakes, rivers, or the ocean? Do you enjoy the sounds of birdsong, insects, and leaves blowing in the breeze? Do you love the scent of flowers, the shape of trees, or breathing in fresh mountain air?

What do you love most about the outdoors?

Whatever answers arise for you, fully immerse yourself in the recollection of them. Make those memories as real as you possibly can by involving all your senses: the sights, smells, tastes, sounds, sensations, and the emotions they evoke.

I invite you to take a moment to savor the experience you just created. Let it be felt on every level of your being. It feels good, right?

As young children, my brother and I spent considerable time at our grandparents' farm in Lancashire. It was a welcome relief from the arguments and tension at home. We loved being with our grandparents because of the freedom it gave us, and they were such loving, kind people.

If it wasn't raining hard, we were turfed outside after breakfast and only allowed to return inside for meals or cooking duties. While I may have grumbled about it then, I'm so grateful to them for this house rule. It forced me to get into the healthy habit of finding something interesting to do and creating adventures while being outside for hours each day. I came to love being outdoors, feeling the weather on my skin, and delighting in the changing seasons.

I spent many blissful hours sitting in the fields, bonding with the calves. They were my dearest friends. I still remember so clearly their smell, the texture of their coarse coats, the feel of their glistening wet noses, and how it felt when they sucked my fingers. To this day, I have a special place in my heart for cows.

My brother and I used to stride about the farm in wellies, filthy, helping with farm jobs that we could manage: mucking out the cow shed, feeding the cows, chickens, and pigeons, collecting eggs for breakfast, and picking blackcurrants for jam making. We dug tunnels in deep snowdrifts and went on expeditions up the "mountain" with Bruce, the loyal, black and white farm dog. We had a brilliant time.

One of my favorite pastimes was sitting on the farm gates, singing my heart out. No wonder the cats often hid in the farmhouse!

My love of the natural world comes from my time on their farm.

As a youngster, I was obsessed with horses and riding. Regardless of the weather, I loved being on horseback in the green, gently rolling countryside of North Yorkshire.

A couple of years ago, I got back on a horse. It was a fabulous experience being out on winding mountain trails in Montana, in a breathtaking landscape with vast blue skies, distant snowcapped mountains, and the fragrant aroma of fir trees on the breeze. It soothed my soul after I'd endured some recent hard knocks in life. The smell of the horses, feeling their warmth underneath me, hearing their grunts, sighs, and snorts, and the sound of their hooves on the logging trails made me beam with happiness inside and out. As we made our way through the foothills, masses of colorful butterflies fluttered by, dancing between the wildflowers. I felt so connected to Mother Nature and easily dropped into her mesmerizing rhythm. It does us the world of good when we spend time outdoors.

I'm passionate about whales and love gazing at the ocean looking for signs of them. During a vacation in gorgeous, verdant Kauai, Hawaii, James and I had seen plenty of spouts, but not a single breach. After a few days, I said to James lightheartedly, "Wouldn't it be amazing to see a complete breach?" but I wasn't particularly attached to it happening. I kid you not, within a few seconds, a whale launched itself clear out of the water right in front of our line of sight! It was the only breach we saw during our vacation.

I'll never know if it was linked to my intention, but it was certainly a bizarre coincidence!

Feeling connected, in whichever ways resonate for us, boosts our health. It feels good and nourishes our souls. A sense of connection can be particularly important for those of us healing from difficult childhoods and feeling somewhat adrift in life.

With luck, my words have inspired you or reminded you of the importance of connection. Perhaps you've even been nudged, ever so gently, to make some adjustments.

# PART 3

# Thriving

# 13

# A COCONUT WITH A MIND OF ITS OWN

Rushing into the living room in a frenzy of enthusiasm and excitement, I clipped my left foot against the metal leg of the coffee table and crashed to the ground.

I'd just come up with a new flow for this book, which felt great! It was around 6 p.m., and I thought, *I've just got time before making dinner to nip into the living room, grab the flip chart I'd scribbled my brilliant ideas on in bright colors, and show it to James.*

As I fell to the floor, my guides exclaimed, *Don't show him! Stop giving away your power.* I was in a lot of pain. My Reiki-trained hands reached for my toe, and I blurted out, "Really?! Was this really necessary?! Couldn't we have sorted this out another way?!"

I protested that I was only going to show him what I had come up with. My guides replied that was true, but then I would have asked him, "What do you think?" They had me there. I would have said exactly that instead of being confident about my own work.

An X-ray the following day confirmed a broken toe. Unbelievably, only one week after my other broken toe had stopped hurting, I found myself facing yet another stint of several weeks with limited mobility. I was intensely disappointed; tears poured down my cheeks, and I felt very sorry for myself for a day or so.

Not trusting my own judgment, seeking approval, and giving away my power were clearly deeply ingrained patterns because it took a broken bone to make me change my ways.

I didn't show my ideas to James, and, in fact, throughout the writing of this book, aside from reading him one brief story about Africa, I haven't dared to show him any of it or ask for his opinion for fear of the repercussions! The Universe had grabbed my attention, and I dove into connecting with my inner guidance and releasing the need for external validation.

I've given away my power freely to family members, some of my friends, most of my lovers, health professionals, healers, intuitives, bosses, and a few teachers.

I'm not alone in this pattern. Many of us repeatedly give away our power to others. Disempowering ourselves can be a pattern formed in childhood to try and keep ourselves safe, and it often continues into adulthood.

Reconnecting to our power, standing up for ourselves, following our inner guidance, and feeling safe to speak our truth all support us on our path to loving ourselves more deeply.

Some of us can be scared to step into our power and speak up because truthfully expressing ourselves resulted in dire consequences in the past. Remember the young Rachel who spoke up at the family meeting? As a family of four, our life was extremely unhealthy and depressing. That younger me knew something had to change. When her dad asked, "Should Mum leave?", Little Rachel knew without a doubt that the best way forward was for her mum to go.

The consequences of her actions were enormous. Her mum moved out, and she was left living with her dad, who didn't take good care of her.

But do you know what? I celebrate that younger me. I'm immensely proud of her. She was a strong, brave, courageous child. She was firmly in her power when she gave her answer. The youngest of the family, she was the only one to declare that something had to change.

For decades afterward, I held back from speaking my truth, silenced myself, and internalized my feelings, which created all kinds of suffering in my life. It's no wonder it was so challenging for me to reclaim my power.

Were there events in your past that contributed to a fear of being in your power? If so, please know that it's possible to heal that aspect of you and live your life knowing it's safe to be in your power.

Calling back our power from the people, places, and things where we've given it away is profoundly healing and beneficial.

We can do this in meditation.

In a quiet, undisturbed moment, relax yourself with some deep breathing and bring your awareness into your heart space. Command to the beloved Divine that you are calling back your power from everywhere that you have handed it out. Envisage it being filtered and purified before re-entering your auric field or body. Feel your power coming back into your energetic system, and sit quietly for a moment, welcoming it back home.

Over the years, I repeatedly gave away my power to my dad. Do you recall the story I shared about the last time I saw him in Cornwall? It was that upsetting, stressful trip that tipped me over the edge, when I managed to stand up to him, reclaiming my power, and enforcing healthy boundaries. We hadn't been in touch for about five months after that horrendous experience.

Well, the story continued. A few months later, my beautiful, musically gifted niece, Charlotte, got married in the idyllic Cotswolds region. We traveled as a clan of six: James and I, along with Jess and her boyfriend, Michael, and Josh and his girlfriend, Anika, from the States to England for the happy occasion.

The instant I laid eyes on my dad, I realized that even though I'd been doing a lot of inner healing work since my Cornish trip, I was still furious with him. We kept out of each other's way.

During the wedding weekend, I shared with my brother what had happened in Cornwall. He listened intently and understood why I was upset. He said that Dad loved me just as much as him, but he couldn't show it. He gently suggested that I make peace with him, as who knew what Dad's destiny held? Something shifted in me as I heard his words.

At breakfast the following morning, I spotted my dad

eating by himself at a table. Nothing unusual about that; he was a loner and preferred it that way. I went over to his table and asked if he wanted to join me, James, and Glenys, my mum's cousin, for breakfast. He agreed. So, I helped move his bits and bobs to our table.

I decided to share with him some lovely memories of my childhood, when we played carols on Christmas morning in our brass trio and some of Grandad Eric's amusing antics. Grandad Eric, his former father-in-law, had been the big character of the family. We had some good laughs as we reminisced. After breakfast, Dad and I said goodbye.

That was the last time I saw him. He died a few days later, alone in his apartment.

I realized after his death that I'd been desperate to get to a place in my life where I could see him and not be triggered by him. And I believed that I'd failed in that regard. But then it dawned on me that Grace had intervened at that breakfast. In addition to the good conversations, there had been a moment when some disparaging behavior flared up in him, but I decided to take the high road and refused to get triggered. I remained calm as I observed with clarity that he simply had an argumentative, difficult personality and was unable to have true, deep, loving relationships with others. I felt a great deal of compassion for him.

So, it turned out that the very last time I saw him, I'd finally managed to stay in my power and had offered an olive branch with love and compassion in my heart. I'm so grateful that my brother's words extinguished my anger and enabled me to make peace with my dad right before he died.

You may or may not be aware that there are energetic cords connecting people. Cords exist in both directions — from us to others, and from them to us. These cords play a crucial role in how we try to gain power, control, or influence and get our needs and desires met. This usually takes place outside our conscious awareness.

Cutting those energetic cords is an excellent ongoing practice that benefits us hugely.

In a meditative state, you can cut the cords to everyone and everything in one go, saving a lot of time. Or you can recall a particular person with whom you're having some issues and ask for all the cords to be cut and removed.

In both cases, you can offer the cut cords to the light rather than returning them to the other person or people. Then, take a moment to fill yourself up with *Divine Love* through the crown of your head before finishing off by sending light and blessings from the Universe to the other.

People can be reluctant to call back their power and cut cords with those they love because they are concerned it will be detrimental to their connection with them. Far from it; instead, it helps us to thrive and strengthens our power, while also cleaning up co-dependency tendencies, all of which improves our relationships with ourselves and others.

It's wise to call back our power and cut cords regularly. Think of it as part of looking after ourselves energetically, like brushing our teeth and flossing.

Be aware that sometimes cords have a habit of re-attaching after you have cut them. This tends to happen if there is a particularly intense, sticky connection or if we have behavior patterns that our soul intends to heal in this lifetime, and we're not getting it. If this happens to you, call in Divine intervention to help you heal whatever is persisting, or ask the Divine to show you the opportunity for learning and evolution so that you can address it and move on.

Reclaiming our power enables us to deepen our connection to our intuition and the Divine. As we listen to our inner nudges and sense of knowingness, and as we trust and follow the guidance and flashes of inspiration that we receive, we continue to stand more fully in our power. With a more conscious and clearer connection to the Divine, we are better able to channel Divine energy through our being, increasing the power available to us for the benefit of all.

It can take a long time for some people to develop and trust this process of listening to their inner wisdom and building a loving connection with the Divine.

After a while, a tipping point is reached, and the energy starts to flow with ease. We begin to automatically trust our intuition, the messages our bodies send us, and our connection to the ultimate source of power, *Love* itself.

Even when this feels natural and easy for us, there are still times when we feel disconnected from Grace and our inner selves. When life kicks up a storm and strong emotions dominate, we can easily find ourselves caught up in our heads, creating a sense of disconnection and powerlessness.

When this happens, and it will now and then, gently close your eyes, take some slow, deep breaths, and exhale any tension. Breathe in spaciousness and calm, or whatever essences would be most beneficial for you, and open to what is untouched by thoughts, emotions, and whatever is occurring in your life. Rest there a while, as you continue to breathe deeply.

Getting out in nature, listening to beautiful music, or moving our bodies can also create an opening to our deeper selves, showing us the way home. Basically, do whatever feels good to you. Experiment and discover your own favorites!

The truth is that our connection to the Divine, the powerful force of *Love*, is always there. It's only our thoughts that make us believe otherwise. So even in our darkest moments, even when we can't sense it, we are always in connection with the Divine. To experience it, all we need to do — and I appreciate it can feel virtually impossible at times — is stop everything we are doing, be still, and let it reveal itself to us.

Be compassionate and patient towards yourself, with great tenderness, and do your best to let go of trying to make it happen. Ironically, we become aware of *Love* when we stop searching for it.

Let it find you.

Many of us diminish our power by making others the authority over ourselves. We listen to their advice rather than our own inner wisdom. It can take considerable courage and persistence to override this pattern. It's a process of trusting if something is a good fit for us by tuning into our inner guidance and acting on what we discover. The more we repeat this, honoring our inner guidance and being our own authority, the stronger we stand in our own power.

It reminds me of an experience I had while healing from my first broken toe. I received advice from a health professional to stop protecting my toe so much and start being more active.

In normal circumstances, I'm a very active person who loves to exercise and keep fit. I can also be very determined, willful, and impatient. With these character traits, I've regularly pushed too hard through injuries and often reinjured myself, worsening the original problem.

However, in this instance, I felt guided to go against my old ways. Instead, I tuned into my body and followed its advice to recover from the break by doing very little.

I honored my body. It was urging me to slow down and rest up for a few weeks. I got the impression it was a life lesson rather than a simple recovery from my broken bone, so I leaned into the opportunity to grow.

I ignored everyone else's opinions about whether I was being overly cautious with my recovery process. In doing so, I realized I'd achieved something rather wonderful. I'd stayed in my power and declared I was the only one who knew what was best for me. I transferred the authority back to its rightful place.

I am the only authority of me.

And you are the only authority of you.

❄

In the summer of 2023, wading through the grief of my dad's sudden death, I was feeling depleted, and I needed a break.

I checked out the upcoming offerings at the Omega Institute of Holistic Studies, near Rhinebeck, New York, just a short drive away from our home.

A weekend retreat led by Tosha Silver, focusing on Radical Gratitude, jumped out at me. I've resonated with her work for many years and love her books and Oracle Cards. Attending one of her retreats felt like a perfect fit for my needs.

I don't know about you, but when I sign up for transformational events, life tends to get a bit chaotic leading up to my departure.

As the weekend approached, I felt progressively off balance energetically. I'd had family staying from the UK for a couple of weeks. It was so lovely to see them, but unfortunately, after a while, I lost my creative groove, and my writing became slow and strained, like wading through thigh-deep mud. I felt agitated because I wasn't progressing sufficiently with my book.

In my creative funk, I found it hard to settle in meditation. My inner world was spinning rapidly, and anxiety about my long to-do list was building. I was behind schedule in writing copy for the new version of my website, and I was feeling demotivated about my YouTube channel.

I was exhausted, deep in the grieving process, and

feeling disconnected from my guides and the Divine.

My heavy state of mind fueled a mini-crisis of confidence about my path and offerings. *What am I doing with my life? Does anyone even find my videos useful? I'm so overwhelmed! This is too hard, and I can't do it all by myself! There just aren't enough hours in the day to get everything done. Writing is so hard for me.* Stressful thoughts were circling like vultures in the sky.

To make matters worse, as I tried to sort out my dad's estate, I was encountering all kinds of difficulties that I couldn't straighten out. And I was struggling to find trustworthy professionals to assist me.

I was fed up and overwhelmed, wishing it would all get sorted out by the wafting around of a magic wand.

Everything seemed to be piling up against me. Nothing was flowing with ease. Even the shower in the master bathroom had leaked that week, causing considerable water damage in our bedroom and the ceiling below. The plumber was missing in action, and the companies I'd contacted to discuss renovating the bathroom were not responding.

So, as I was saying, a storm was blowing through in the weeks before the retreat!

Tosha had instructed us to bring a coconut with milk sloshing around inside, a cup of sea salt, and a beautiful item to give away.

The perfect thing came to mind. I had bought a gorgeous necklace a few years prior, but whenever I wore it, I sensed it belonged to someone else. I knew it was meant to find its new owner at the retreat. I packed up my belongings and drove to the Omega Institute, ready for a weekend of transformation in beautiful, tranquil surroundings.

I dove into the world of radical gratitude, which is centered on thanking everything we experience in our lives, the totality of our existence — the wonderful things along with the most painful events, and everything in between.

During the weekend, we thanked the brilliant things in our lives — a breeze! My loving relationship with James, my kids, my dog, my friends, my health, the gorgeous summer's day, my beautiful home — the list went on. With so many wonderful things to be grateful for, it reminded me how fortunate I truly am.

We moved onto thanking the trickier feelings and events. I immersed myself in the raw grief about my dad's death, the difficulties with sorting out his estate, the overwhelm, agitation, and frustration that were circling around, together with the crisis of confidence about my offerings and general direction in life. I graciously thanked all of it.

We were guided through clearing out the beliefs and emotions that had surfaced. The vibration of the whole group was on the rise.

It felt amazing to be with courageous people committed to improving their lives by freeing themselves from painful events and stubborn, limiting beliefs. They were my kind of people. Massive transformations were occurring within our group.

Keen to connect with my deeper self during the retreat,

I devoted a significant amount of time to silence in the meditation hall. In doing so, I discovered that my connection to the Divine was right there, despite what I'd been telling myself to the contrary. It hadn't gone anywhere. *Love* was constant and unchanging regardless of my mental state. I realized that my frantic state of mind — the overwhelm and stressful thoughts — had led me to believe I was disconnected from Grace. I was reminded that it's impossible to be disconnected, merely distracted. All that's required is to let go of our thoughts and drop our stories as we fall inside in silence. My energy relaxed and slowed down. I felt calm, loved, soothed, nurtured, and replenished, enabling me to be fully present to the whole experience of the retreat.

Are you curious about the coconuts and sea salt?

A coconut-smashing ceremony was scheduled for the final day of the retreat. Smashing coconuts is a powerful way of breaking through our persistent obstacles, releasing painful limiting beliefs, and shattering our illusions. It sets us free from their tenacious grip and enables us to transform our lives.

As directed, we'd been transmitting all our thoughts, emotions, and situations that we wanted to release to our hairy coconuts. I spoke tenderly to mine, gently whispering my thoughts into its cells until it became saturated with everything I was done with.

In preparation for the ceremony, we showered and scrubbed our bodies with sea salt to purge unwanted energies from our bodies and energy fields.

Sea salt scrub ... done; putting my troublesome thoughts into my coconut ... done. I was ready.

On the last morning of the retreat, our soulful group of fifty-six people went outside to pulverize our coconuts.

We were asked to remain silent throughout the ceremony until we returned to the meeting room.

Standing in a circle around some large, flat concrete structures in the grass, Tosha instructed us on the necessary steps. When you feel guided to take your turn, step forward to the center of the circle, vividly imagine what you want to release, raise your coconut up high, firmly holding it in both hands, and smash it down hard onto the concrete. Easy.

Tosha warned us that sometimes issues could be stubborn and persistent, and they might be reluctant to leave. This meant that occasionally, it could take several attempts before the coconut broke open. If that happened, no worries. Stay in the middle of the circle and continue throwing until your coconut smashes into pieces.

It was a gorgeous, warm summer morning in early July. The sun was shining, and clouds were dancing through the bright blue sky. Our tribe of soulful beings stood in a large circle on the lush green grass with the concrete structures in the center. As each of us felt an inner calling, we migrated to the circle's center, thought about what we wanted to release, raised our coconut high above our heads, and threw it down with tremendous power. Most broke on the first impact; others took a couple of throws.

After about ten people had completed their release

ritual, I felt compelled to go next. I moved into the center, raised my coconut high above my head, gripped it tightly, recalled all the things I wanted to release — the grief, frustration, overwhelm, and self-doubt — and slammed it down onto the concrete. My coconut hit the structure and ricocheted, completely unblemished, straight through the other side of the circle at lightning speed. A gap opened up as people scattered to avoid a direct hit!

"That's a tricky little coconut," I muttered aloud as I strode off to find it on the far side of the circle. "I've got you this time," I whispered to it as I returned to the center for my second throw. Determined to smash it into smithereens, I lifted my hairy friend high in the air and thrust my arms down with great force. It bounced off at impressive speed in a different direction, and just like the first time, my coconut flew straight through the ring of nervous onlookers.

As I wandered off to retrieve my coconut for the second time, noting its stubborn resistance to breakage, I heard a loud male voice say, "Are you sure you want to release that?" So much for honoring the silence for our sacred ceremony. The second I heard his comment, it was as if someone had thrown petrol on a fire. I was incandescently furious, and the words "You motherfucker" slipped quietly out of my mouth.

Suddenly, I was filled with astronomical levels of powerful energy. In a flash, I was charged with all the times I'd been belittled, silenced or dismissed, told I was wrong, or treated unkindly or disrespectfully by men throughout my life. Over the years, I'd been on the receiving end of hurtful comments and actions from male family members, lovers, teachers, colleagues, and bosses. Even strangers and men I barely knew had directed these unpleasant traits towards me; all of them had stung, and I felt diminished whenever it happened. In that instant, I raged inside; I'd had more than enough of this thoughtless, disparaging behavior.

I retrieved my coconut, which had only sustained a minor crack, and strode back into the center with great purpose. With every step I took, I called forth all the hurts, injustices, and struggles from those interactions with men. As I hurled my coconut against the concrete circle for the third time, I unloaded my fury and shouted, "Fuck you!" as I slammed it down. My coconut exploded, virtually evaporating into the ether.

I felt a deafening internal roar, an explosion of liberation, as I freed up my power that had been diminished for eons. I was acutely aware that I was releasing this not only for myself in this lifetime but also for my lineage, my ancestors, my daughter, my nieces, my grandniece, and those women who will come after me. The impact burned through my past lives and way out into the female collective. A massive release was taking place.

Crackling with power, I returned to my place in the circle with colossal levels of energy coursing through my body. It felt like I was plugged into the electricity supply; my body shook uncontrollably. My feet were deeply rooted into the ground, an integral part of the immense life force of the natural world. I could feel the magnificent power of Mother Earth flowing through every cell in my being.

It took a long while for this powerful energy to settle down enough so that I could come back into my body,
returning to be fully present in the circle.

When everyone had broken their coconuts, we walked
back to the meeting room in silence. Tosha invited us to
share our experience if we so wished. Even though I was
still furious about what had happened, I decided not to
share with the group.

I didn't want to be rude about the man who had spoken
to me or shame him in front of everyone. I was reluctant to
drag the energy of misogyny into the retreat. It just didn't
feel right. So, I sat in the meeting room and listened to others convey their experiences.

As the sharing segment neared completion, I noticed a
familiar sensation bubbling up inside me. My Higher Self
wanted me to speak to the group as something important
to my evolution was about to occur.

I shook my head with great dismay; dread surged
through my body, and I felt acutely uncomfortable. But I
knew only too well from past experiences that there was
only one way to calm the storm: I had to share with the
group. My self-talk was awash with fearful thoughts like
*No! I don't want to speak up. I don't want to bring that sex-
ist dynamic into the retreat. I don't even know what to say
or how to begin. I don't want the attention on me. Please
don't make me do this!*

Something quite miraculous happened as these persistent thoughts swirled around in my inner universe. A massive shift occurred, and radical gratitude washed through

every level of my being. I realized the gratitude was for the man who had spoken up when I was attempting to smash my coconut. Well, I certainly hadn't seen that coming. My anger and hurt dissolved, and they were replaced by *Love*.

As I sat silently thanking him, I realized it was this pattern with men that I'd most needed to release. I'd had enough of being dismissed, rejected, abandoned, belittled, silenced, treated with a lack of respect, and shamed by men. I'd come to the retreat believing that other things needed to be cleared from my energetic system, but this total stranger had shown me otherwise. No wonder my coconut had made its escape twice! It had been holding out for him to show me exactly what was ready to be cleared.

My hand went into the air as if it was being raised by the Divine, and Tosha invited me to speak.

I began by saying that I had no idea who the man was who had spoken up when I couldn't break my coconut, and I added that I didn't need to know. I'd written his exact words in my journal and read them aloud. Right then, a man sheepishly raised his hand and remained silent. I looked him in the eye and nodded at him with respect and confidence. I spoke directly to him and told him that I was enormously grateful to him for saying what he did, and I meant it because he'd shown me so clearly what lay at the core of what I had most needed to release from my life.

I spoke to the group briefly about how men had mistreated me throughout my life and that I was sick of it. Breaking the coconut had been such a powerful release of that energy and the beliefs that were tied to it. I let them all know that I felt empowered and didn't regard myself as a victim in any shape or form. I shared that immense energy had been liberated and was surging through my veins.

When I finished speaking, a round of applause filled the room. Several people approached me afterward. Women said they'd experienced the same from men and knew how it felt; others said they were sorry that I'd been treated that way by men. The woman who sat next to me shared that she was furious when the man spoke during the ceremony and had felt extremely protective towards me. Men came up and expressed they couldn't believe the guy acted that way towards me.

I heard their words, and I felt their love and compassion. I truly did. I received it all, soaking it in. But what I recall most strongly from that moment is the love and compassion I felt for myself; I sensed my strong connection to the Divine and the integration taking place deep within.

I had reclaimed my power.

I knew my life had changed, that the shackles were off. I'd released myself, regained my self-esteem and self-respect, and fallen more deeply into loving myself.

If you're wondering about the necklace I brought to give away, I'm happy to share that it found its new home. A charming woman I chatted with at the beginning of the retreat saw me place my necklace on the gifting table. During the gift exchange, she walked towards me with a huge smile on her face, dangling the necklace in front of me. She was ecstatic and said with glee that she loved my energy and was thrilled it was still there when she went up to select her gift. Perfect!

Nothing called to me when I perused the objects on the gift table. My guides shared that I wasn't meant to take a physical object home because I'd received what I came for. The gift had come from the man who broke the silence and showed me what to focus on. That was the most valuable gift of all. Thank you, beloved soul friend.

What a potent transformational weekend at Omega. Radical gratitude indeed!

We are not victims of our circumstances; we are powerful co-creators of our reality, and we get to choose how we respond to life.

Nobody can take away our power unless we give it to them.

In victim mentality, we are powerless, at the mercy of others and events. When we own our power, we have the ability to change our lives for the better.

In doing so, we enter into the energetic flow of life-force energy — into *Love*, the true powerhouse, where miracles can occur.

Reclaim your power, dear beloved!

# 14

# BREADCRUMBS
# SOAKED IN BLISS

The energy of bliss vibrates at the same frequency as *Love*, which is our true essence — our True Self — as a droplet of *Love*. When we follow our bliss, we tend to have extraordinary experiences, and our lives become rich and truly wonderful.

Contrary to popular belief, vast sums of money and elevated status rarely bring true, deep fulfillment or a sense of profound bliss. Even with tremendous wealth and power, people can have fears about scarcity — believing there just isn't enough to go around, that they always need more, or that they will never have enough. Fear of losing their stash, status, or power is commonplace. At its extreme, they can become paranoid, distrusting others and insisting everyone is out to get them. I know people like that, and it's a painful way to live.

Let's take a jaunt into the world of bliss.

We discover true bliss by connecting with ourselves deep inside and paying attention to what our body communicates via felt sensations.

It's easy to misinterpret what is meant by following our bliss. We can believe it's about indulging ourselves or eating heaps of dessert or pizza every night if we feel like it. Please know I'm not saying you should or shouldn't do anything. Do what you like! The point I'm making is that the bliss I'm referring to lies deeper than satisfying those kinds of desires.

Sometimes, following our bliss feels fantastic, and then there are times when something deep inside us calls us to follow a particular path that feels scary or very challenging. It isn't always comfortable or easy to follow our bliss, but it can take us on a journey of incredible healing, self-discovery, and growth.

What brings you immense pleasure and joy? What makes your heart expand and truly delights you? If you could do anything, what would it be? Let yourself be expansive as you do this. See what arises in your mind's eye.

When we spend time doing things that energize us and make us feel fabulous, when we visit places or live where it feels good to us, and when we spend time with people who nourish our souls and delight us, we're in alignment with our true nature, our Higher Self. By following our bliss, we boost our body's innate ability to heal itself, and we thrive big time.

Being brave enough to follow the breadcrumbs soaked in bliss, one step at a time, and regularly stopping to check in with our inner compass, transforms our lives in powerful ways. It raises our vibration. And as we listen to our guidance, we build and strengthen a loving relationship with our intuition, which responds by sending us clearer and more frequent messages.

Following our bliss can be as simple as roller skating, crafting, listening to beautiful music, taking a relaxing bath, calling a good friend, reading at the beach, meditating, or cuddling with our furry friends.

When we are caught up in our heads, believing there just isn't enough time to get things done, we often avoid taking good care of ourselves. We may ignore the signs our bodies send us and regard doing things we enjoy as decadent, unimportant, or selfish.

You may be wondering how to determine what is blissful for you. Or perhaps you're pondering how to connect with that blissful state of being to guide you through the ups and downs of life.

One brilliant way of checking our bliss barometer is to bring our awareness into our bodies and observe the sensations we notice within us. Tapping into our bodies and how they respond when we consider different possibilities helps us sense if our activities, location, and relationships are blissful, and in alignment with our True Self. They also indicate if we are moving towards or away from our soul's purpose.

You'll recall from Chapter 6 that this highly valuable practice, which is so useful in our everyday lives, involves employing all of our senses to notice physical sensations ranging from intense to incredibly subtle.

Simply put, things that are in alignment with bliss feel good — maybe a pleasant buzz, a feeling of expansion or spaciousness, or a level of excitement. In contrast, situations, activities, and relationships that are not blissful to us often feel heavy, dense, flat, tight, or painful. Those are just examples, though. Take some time to recall a few things from your past that were fabulous experiences, and pretend that they are happening right now. Pay attention to how your body responds and the similarities in sensations. What are your body's signals for bliss — your "Hell yes!"?

Then repeat the process for situations or relationships that were unpleasant or a poor fit for you. Remember to imagine that they're occurring right now, in this instant. Then you'll also know how your body speaks to you when something isn't a good fit for you, which is the same as your "no" response.

This trustworthy internal guidance system is always available to us. Accessing it is simple: we just need to tune in and sense how our bodies respond to what is happening or what we are considering.

Bliss can also show up as a deep knowing or certainty, a sense of the Universe speaking Truth to us. It can feel as though we are responding to a deep calling. You might feel compelled to take action even if you are feeling daunted or scared; this often signifies that the Universe is nudging us into action. This feels noticeably different from your strong "no" response. Trust that you can tell the difference when this occurs.

When this arises for me, I sense an expansion in my heart (my "yes" sensation). A strong sense of certainty accompanies it, and yet, at the same time, there is some mild tension right at the top of my throat. As I breathe deeply and lean into it, the certainty strengthens, which helps me trust that I am correctly understanding my deeper guidance.

Become familiar with these sets of signals, your "yes" and "no" responses. Use them regularly to help you make decisions. As I mentioned in a previous chapter, start with small choices to gain confidence and trust in the process before graduating to more significant decisions.

Then, apply this approach to what is happening in your daily life, as it occurs, and when considering a particular idea. Discover how your inner guidance responds to your actions and thoughts. Following the positive sensations will steer you onto the path of what is truly in alignment with you. This is how we can gauge whether we are heading towards or away from our True Self's desires for this lifetime.

The more you practice, the easier it will become, and you will become delightfully fluent in your body's language, effortlessly noticing what feels good to you and resonates with your heart.

I've learned the hard way that doing things out of resonance with our True Self tends to cause us issues. We dim our incredible light and can find ourselves adrift in life, moving away from what our soul truly desires. Repeatedly disregarding our bliss over long periods of time and acting out of alignment with our deeper selves often contributes to the emergence of health issues. I firmly believe that there is an energetic component to every ailment or injury in the body.

An integral part of loving and honoring ourselves is regularly checking in with our inner barometer to see how our True Self feels about things, rather than what our egoic personality fancies doing.

When we find ourselves heading in the wrong direction, instead of being harsh or self-critical, pause for a moment, take some deep breaths, and then readjust your course by following whatever resonates in that moment. It might be as simple as having a cup of your favorite tea or going for a walk. That breadcrumb will help to reorientate you, acting like a reset button that will lead you to the next breadcrumb, which will lead you to the next one. One step at a time. It really is that simple. Keep in touch with your inner navigation system; it will become your dearest friend, helping you live a happy and fulfilled life.

It's very common for our hobbies and interests to shift when we are on a spiritual journey, even when our egos stubbornly resist the change. Sometimes, the Universe steers us in a new direction that is more aligned with our Higher Selves.

When we lived in North Carolina, I was a keen tennis player and played on United States Tennis Association (USTA) teams. Tennis took up a lot of my time each week, and I was obsessed with it. I played for fun with friends and engaged in USTA matches, team practices, and private lessons. Playing tennis fueled my competitive nature and encouraged my aggressive streak. "You're going down, sweet sister!"

I didn't realize it then, but the identity of "tennis Rachel" conflicted with my spiritual practice.

So, it probably won't come as a surprise to you that the Universe intervened. My right calf sustained three consecutive injuries while I was playing. Each injury was more severe than the previous one, and the last involved a torn plantaris muscle. The torn muscle stopped me in my tracks and caused agonizing pain. It took a long time to heal, giving me an opportunity to ponder what was happening.

I hadn't been listening to my inner guidance. I'd been so determined to keep playing, with my competitive ego taking control, that I'd ignored the signs my body was giving me. It had to shout loudly, in the form of an excruciating injury, for me to finally listen.

Although I knew that the Divine was steering me away from tennis, I was extremely reluctant to stop. So, as soon as I had sufficiently recovered, I tentatively and half-heartedly returned to the tennis court. Nervous about reinjuring myself, I wasn't playing well. As a doubles player, that wasn't fair to my tennis partners. Playing tennis had lost its appeal.

So, I gave up tennis.

*Okay, Universe, so tennis is off the cards; what is my next step?* I tuned into what was lit up for me and felt guided to improve my oil painting skills instead.

As I mentioned in Chapter 11, painting gives me immense joy and a sense of fulfillment. While creating artwork, I'm in the flow and connected to the Divine. Diving into my painting unleashed my passion and sensuality and helped me to release stored-up painful emotions from my past. Art facilitated profound healing in me and became an important part of my healing journey into loving myself.

I came to see that tennis had been very ego-based for me. It didn't feel wonderful, except when I made great shots or we won our matches. Most of the time, it was stressful and slightly obsessive.

No wonder the Divine redirected me into painting and out of tennis!

When considering which country, town, or house to live in, it's very helpful to tune into our body's language and make decisions based on its signals.

Relocating to Charlotte in 2011 was a great career move for James and took the pressure off our family financially. We discovered that it was a very convenient place to live, and the cost of living was much more reasonable than in New Jersey. Charlotte has superb restaurants, a fabulous choice of exercise studios, local big sports teams, loads of opportunities to attend amazing concerts at sensible prices, a thriving artistic community, excellent medical facilities, and an international airport. What's not to like?!

Well, there were plenty of great things about the city, but the climate did not agree with me, and I didn't resonate with the energy of the land.

It was so hot and humid for extended periods each year, and due to its geographical location, there was rarely a breeze. I felt like I was suffocating, as if I couldn't breathe properly. With exceptionally fair English skin, I had to limit my outdoor time, and to make matters worse, I get irritable when I overheat! I missed spending lots of time outdoors. It was miserable for me, and I felt imprisoned for most of the year. Despite Charlotte's plus points, it turned out to be a tough place to live harmoniously.

When our youngest was in his senior year of high school, James decided to look for a new job. As employment options in the financial sector are more plentiful in New York City, we decided to return to the Northeast.

I focused my search on Westchester County, New York, and southern Connecticut. My friend Krysta told me she loved the Connecticut coastal town of Westport and suggested I check it out.

I drove to Compo Beach in Westport on one of my house-hunting trips. Huge, gray granite boulders sat regally on the beach. They were calling to me, so I went over to sit on one. Wrapped up snugly in winter clothing, with snow on the beach, I closed my eyes, took some deep breaths, and brought my awareness into my heart space.

When I felt clear and centered, I asked if Westport was a good fit for me as a hometown. In response, I felt an almighty buzz and tingling of energy in my body — a loud "yes!"

Based on my inner guidance, we focused our search

on Westport.

While searching for a house with a great art studio space, I viewed over forty properties. I relied on how my body felt energetically inside each one. My realtor was a little frustrated sometimes when, five minutes after walking into a property, immediately sensing it was a poor match vibrationally, I'd leave and move on to the next house! The instant I laid eyes on our house on realtor.com, I knew it was our new home. I flew up to see it; James viewed it two days later, and my body gave me the thumbs up, so we bought it.

Following my bliss led me to this stunningly beautiful New England town. I genuinely love living here. Being so close to the ocean feels amazing. There's a breeze! The stone walls remind me of England. With an interesting blend of American and international residents, it's my favorite place to live in America so far.

When I graduated from university at twenty-one, I moved to Brighton, on the English south coast. I rented a teeny-tiny one-bedroom apartment, a leisurely five-minute stroll from the beach. After work, when the weather was decent, I'd pick up my mail and pop over to the pebble beach to open it, soaking in the sights, sounds, and smells of the sea and beach, feeling so lucky to be living there. It was the first time I'd lived by the sea, and I was smitten.

Jumping back to my Connecticut relocation: In choosing to return to coastal living, I've reconnected with that younger part of me. And that feels outrageously good.

Walking by the ocean, kayaking, cycling along the coastal road, watching sunsets on the beach, and admiring the rise of full moons over the Long Island Sound, all light me up inside. When I'm having a tough time, walking by the ocean or sitting on the beach with my bare hands or feet in the sand always soothes my soul, and I return home feeling rebalanced, nourished, and peaceful.

I love kayaking. During the summer months, I go out into the Long Island Sound as much as I can, laughing and chatting with my kayaking buddies. I dip my fingers into the clear, blue water, watching my hands swirl around in the ocean and loving the sound that makes. I never tire of watching the local wildlife as I absorb the breathtakingly gorgeous surroundings. I am beyond grateful for living in such a wonderful place that feels so harmonious to my heart and soul.

I even like that it can be a little unnerving when I'm paddling against a strong current or tide or when we are reminded of the delicate nature of our human form. A few years ago, my family of four was paddling in the deep, cold Pacific Ocean off the coast of Monterey, California. We found ourselves uncomfortably close to a shark enthusiastically killing and devouring a seal. That got my heart racing, but strangely, it also made me feel full of the vitality and richness of life. And it gave us an excellent story to tell afterward!

❁

It's early spring here in New England, and I just got back from riding my bike. I was lucky enough to cycle past glorious displays of bright yellow daffodils, white and purple crocuses, and heavily scented pink hyacinths as I huffed and puffed around my one-hour coastal route. Two of my favorite things at once: Cycling and being by the ocean. Pure heaven on earth!

How did you learn to ride a bike when you were a child?

I learned with my dad running alongside me on a tarmac residential street, pushing me downhill with great enthusiasm and gusto. After propelling me forward, he stood back and cheered me on, celebrating my successes.

As a youngster, I cycled with my dad and brother on Sunday afternoons. Off the three of us went on mini-adventures. In the late summer, we picked wild blackberries from the hedgerows for mum to make an apple and blackberry crumble. My dad always said I had a keen eye for ripe blackberries.

Cycling was my primary mode of transport in my teenage years. I cycled in and out of Winchester, to and from my friends' houses. It gave me a vital sense of freedom and independence. Sometimes, I still dream about the route between Winchester and my house in Kings Worthy. The dreams are so vivid and real. Riding my bike past the watercress beds in Headbourne Worthy, pedaling along underneath the railway bridge, and past the bus stops. I knew it like the back of my hand.

I adore cycling. It's been a constant presence in my life and is still my favorite thing to do. Being outside gives me such a boost, feeling the weather against my face on any given day. I celebrate all the seasons as they come and go.

Cycling is immensely comforting to me. It is an essential touchstone in my life. My body is so familiar with the motions, and the bike feels like an extension of me. Brilliant insights often drift into my mind while I'm on a ride, and I'm often blessed with new ways of seeing a problem in my life.

I used to hate it when other cyclists tried to overtake me. I pushed myself as hard as I could, ignoring my screaming thighs! That old me was determined to stay ahead. Not only was I competitive with others but also with myself, always trying to better my circuit times.

I've long since given up on timing myself. And these days, I honestly couldn't care less if someone overtakes me. I'm focusing on listening to my body, exercising, soaking in the sights and sounds, and enjoying every single moment of my ride. Perhaps this more relaxed attitude is a side effect of having been on a spiritual path for so long. Who knows?

When I need fresh air and a break from writing, painting, or working with clients, I love getting changed into my cycling clothes, pumping up my tires, putting on my helmet, switching on my flashing lights, hopping onto my bike, and heading out onto the road.

Cycling is a blissful activity for me. When I get back

from a ride, I feel invigorated and renewed. I receive an almighty reboot to my whole energetic system. It puts a smile in my heart and on my face.

I feel a comforting connection with my dad and brother through cycling. It links me to them in a positive, fun way, as it was the one thing we all enjoyed. With the cycling bug still at play, my mind naturally focuses on joy rather than the challenging difficulties we faced in our relationships. My dad gave me a precious gift by encouraging me to cycle as a child. Thank you, Dad.

What do you delight in doing? And are you making time for it? What energizes you and opens up your intuition?

In 2008, while attending my NLP Master Practitioner Course in Lake Las Vegas, Nevada, the trainers told us about the next level of training: a four-week NLP Trainers Training Certification program, where we would be taught how to become great presenters and learn how to train others in NLP.

I enjoyed studying NLP and was very keen to take the training. They offered us two options: Lake Las Vegas or Sydney, Australia.

I was turning forty in the year the training was taking place. When they mentioned Sydney, every cell in my body lit up with excitement and delight. It sounded like a bold, daring move with a huge helping of adventure. I saw it as a fantastic opportunity to visit Australia, a country

I'd longed to see, and I'd get certified as a trainer of NLP. What a fabulous way to celebrate my fortieth birthday year!

We were tight for money back then, so James wasn't keen on my plans. He told me that if I wanted to go to Australia, I'd have to earn the money to pay for it. I rose to the challenge and did that with ease.

To make my dream possible, I needed to make childcare arrangements. Jess and Josh were twelve and ten years old at the time. James and my mum, who flew over from the UK, stepped up to look after the kids in my absence. All the details fell into place, and off I flew to Australia.

My time in Sydney was one of the most incredible experiences of my life to date. I loved the city. I soaked in the climate and the sounds of birds and insects and adored the unfamiliar plants. There was even a moment of high alert when I freaked out at a spider on the ceiling of my hotel room. I called the hotel staff to come and remove it, in case it was a poisonous Sydney funnel-web spider! Thankfully, it was a false alarm!

The course was intense and thorough. The instructors put us through our paces. We only had four days off during the month and even worked through weekends. My evenings were spent writing presentations and practicing them for the next day. I dug deep and came up with diamonds. It was an enjoyable, fulfilling, and satisfying experience.

It was thrilling to be in Sydney. I even managed to fit in spending the day with a first cousin once removed, Stephen, whom I'd never met. He is on my Grandad Eric's side of the family. What a kind, generous, lovely man! It was a little disconcerting though, because some of Stephen's mannerisms reminded me of my grandad. Genes are fascinating sometimes.

I also spent time with a couple of old friends from my Winchester days. One of them, Steve, lives in Sydney, and Pete was visiting him from China. I hadn't seen either of them in over twenty years. It was good for my soul to see them, and we shared a lot of laughs.

It still fills me with joy when I remember my Australian adventure. I acted on that lit-up feeling, followed my bliss, and booked my course and trip. It turned out to be a fantastic experience that challenged me and helped me grow. I returned to the USA more confident, believing in myself more than ever before, and feeling incredibly empowered.

When I trained as a Pilates instructor in 2005, I discovered how effective Pilates can be in helping people heal injuries and muscular imbalances.

A few years ago, some niggling physical issues began to bother me and were restricting my activities. Yoga seemed to be aggravating my body. My shoulders, lower back, and hips were shouting at me. So, I decided to find a good Pilates teacher to see if the exercises would help my body regain a healthy balance. I signed up for private classes at a local studio.

In my haste to get moving, I followed a friend's recommendation and forgot to check my selection with my inner self. I discovered that the studio focused on a strict and rigid methodology. My body wasn't responding well, and I noticed a persistent reluctance to attend my sessions, but I was keen to please the teacher, so I pushed myself forward. Instead of improving my injuries, it made them worse.

Even though my body wasn't making progress, she reassured me that in the longer term, it would help to sort out my problems. All the while, I was ignoring what my body was trying to tell me. I felt like a round peg trying to squeeze into a triangular hole, but I believed her and kept showing up for class.

After several months, I started to feel hopeless about the state of my body. I was going backward, and my body was hurting. To make matters worse the teacher mentioned my mild scoliosis every time I saw her. I felt deformed and demoralized.

During a Rolfing session, my practitioner, Sharon, was working on releasing tension from my latest Pilates session. Never one to beat around the bush, she asked me in a confused and exasperated fashion why on earth I continued to do something my body didn't like.

At that moment, something clicked. Sharon had a good point! So, when I got home, I canceled my remaining Pilates appointments.

By searching online and carefully checking reviews, I found another Pilates studio, Black Rock Pilates. My inner guidance gave it a big thumbs up, so I signed up for classes.

What a brilliant move that was. I'd trusted and acted on the blissful feeling inside me, and in doing so, my body improved by leaps and bounds. Their instructors are extremely knowledgeable and have a flexible approach. I love being a part of their community; it's a welcoming, relaxed, and friendly place.

To make it even sweeter, the studio owner, Laura, introduced me to Catherine, the most gifted muscle whisperer I've ever met. Listening to my inner guidance led me to her intuitive, knowledgeable, sparkly self. Her presence in my life has enabled me to heal a multitude of old emotional, physical, and mental wounds, and I adore spending time with her.

Following what feels joyful and lit up in our careers and in all the ways we're of service is another essential component of living in alignment with our Higher Self.

If we have a job that we dislike or is extremely stressful, or if we're working in a toxic environment, or perhaps all three, it has a pronounced detrimental effect on our mental, emotional, physical, and spiritual selves. We can lose touch with who we are at our core and find ourselves miserable, unwell, and feeling stuck.

After a few decades of working for top-tier banks, James's soul was shouting at him to break free and make significant changes in his life.

He attended a men's retreat in South Africa and had a profound breakthrough. On his return, he started carving stones, and we discovered that he's an extremely gifted sculptor. James signed up for a coaching certification course and pondered what he enjoyed that might bring him true meaning and fulfillment. Several months later, during an organizational change at work, he decided he'd had enough and quit.

His inner guidance was nudging him to explore new life opportunities and focus on self-care. The result? He's feeling relieved and much happier. He's enjoying a healthier balance in his life as he envisions what he'd like to do next. Recently, he spent a couple of weeks in the heart of Kruger National Park, South Africa — his happy place — learning how to track wild animals on foot with Renias Mhlongo, a world-renowned master tracker. Renias's presence and wisdom inspire profound transformations, reminding us of the deep connections we share with the natural world and each other.

I have tremendous respect for people who listen to their hearts and are brave enough to make bold changes in their careers towards what elicits joy for them. Walking away from jobs and careers takes tremendous courage. Expectations of ourselves, anxiety about what others will think of us, loss of status, fear of the unknown, and fears of scarcity can hold us back from following the path our soul longs for us to take.

If we wish to continue with our existing job or career, paying attention to how we feel about its various aspects and focusing on the things that feel good and expansive tend to guide us towards a wonderfully fulfilling path.

With my own business activities, I regularly check in to

determine how I resonate with existing offerings and new ideas. If something no longer feels lit up, I reorient myself to what feels in alignment.

When something isn't feeling blissful, we may have uncovered limiting beliefs that are holding us back, or it may mean that we need to take a whole new direction or that it's simply an issue of timing. Perhaps we're being asked to press pause and turn our attention to something else for a while, trusting that we'll know when we're meant to return to the original task or project.

Tuning in to our body's signals and taking action based on what we discover helps us navigate our careers and businesses. Go easy on yourself, though, because this way of living requires great courage and trust.

Has this ever happened to you? Sometimes, we follow the energized, joyful feeling, and it leads us down problematic paths. We can end up doubting our intuition and wondering what the heck happened. Recognize this as a golden opportunity to lean in and trust that it is part of the learning and expansion experience.

Very often, the toughest challenges present us with the greatest evolution and, in the longer term, tend to propel us towards a remarkable life — even if it's a struggle along the way.

I've become better at running my business in alignment with my inner guidance. With people-pleasing tendencies and a predisposition to make others the authority, it's been a long journey to get comfortable trusting my inner compass instead of doing as others think I should.

I give myself permission to look after my own needs. By doing that, I am loving myself. I only post on social media when I'm genuinely moved to do so, and I go at a harmonious pace rather than buying into the workaholic mindset. Getting depleted and exhausted is not loving myself, and I know I'm of limited value to others when I don't take care of myself first.

After listening to an inner spark of playfulness, I created a YouTube channel (@RachelJaneLinnett). However, before launching it, I procrastinated for over a year because I was nervous about becoming more visible. A swarm of pesky limiting beliefs buzzed around: *No one will want to watch me. I have nothing valuable to say. I can't relax in front of the camera.* Tired of my excuses, I decided to hold myself accountable by joining a group of women who were working with a visibility coach, in the hope that participating would nudge me into action.

I was ready to bloom. Two weeks in, I launched my YouTube adventure. To my surprise and delight, I discovered that recording and sharing videos with the world is a lot of fun. It's like hanging out with my dearest friends, sharing some stories, inspiration, wisdom, and laughter, offering powerful, energetic transmissions, and assisting people in transforming their lives.

I love supporting people on a journey of healing and transformation. Interwoven through my various offerings are the enjoyment and fulfillment of guiding others to the stillness and *Love* at their core. It's such an honor to be a catalyst in their healing journey as they free themselves from painful, limiting thoughts and stubborn, dense emotions. And what a joy it is to witness them as they improve their lives by following their inner guidance.

Always remember that following our bliss applies to the small things as well as the bigger ones.

On a day when you feel overwhelmed or lose your way, be gentle to yourself and ask what small step you can take to love and support yourself.

What simple thing can you do in your day that would feel great? Answer from the place inside you that wants the absolute best for you.

Perhaps it's going for a walk, preparing a delicious meal, or starting a new project that inspires you. It might be giving yourself permission to take a nap if you feel exhausted, putting your to-do list aside, or signing up for an interesting training course, or booking a vacation to somewhere you've always wanted to visit. Only you know what tickles your fancy. Tune in and follow through.

Whatever it is, make time for yourself. You are important, valuable, and lovable just as you are, and you deserve to take the time to look after yourself.

Engaging in what we love raises our vibration and helps us to advance in the direction our soul wants us to travel in this lifetime.

Whether it's hobbies, careers, where we live, or who we spend time with: listen intently to your inner nudges, and follow what energizes you and lights you up in some way. As you take action, your life will be enhanced in the most magnificent ways.

Be brave, dear soul friend, surrender to *Love*, and let *Love* take the lead in your life.

Above all else, give yourself full permission to love yourself.

# EPILOGUE

As this book draws to a close, I have one last tale for you about a complete circle interwoven with beautiful synchronicities.

As a young woman in my mid-twenties, I began to realize that I suffered from chronic low self-esteem. Immense unworthiness was circling around inside me, coupled with an exceedingly unhealthy response to stressful situations. I didn't feel good about myself or know what to do about it.

Back then, I wasn't consciously aware of the extent to which my childhood had shaped and adversely impacted my life. Sure, I knew it hadn't been a great upbringing, to say the least. But instead of dwelling on the negativity, I'd focused on surviving, pushing through, being tough, and expertly avoiding my emotional wounds.

A negative experience with a child psychologist at fourteen made me distrust therapy, so I didn't believe it could help me, even when I was struggling.

In my twenties, I wasn't ready to explore healing from my traumatic past, but I wanted to find a way to improve my life. Deep down, I knew a better way of existing was possible, and I longed to feel better about myself.

Driven by a strong urge to improve things, I browsed the shelves of a local bookstore, searching for a book that might offer some easy solutions. I came across *Don't Sweat the Small Stuff — and It's All Small Stuff: Simple Ways to*

*Keep the Little Things from Taking Over Your Life*, by Richard Carlson. I knew it was the book I was meant to read, so I bought it.

I devoured his book at great pace and loved every single word. Reading it helped me feel I wasn't alone in my predicament. Someone else had gone to the trouble of writing a book to help others reduce stress levels and live happier lives. What a star!

That book was the first self-help book I'd read, and it was precisely what I needed at that time.

It's funny how things happen sometimes — the flow of our lives, the synchronicities. Almost three decades after reading Richard Carlson's book, an amazing series of events brought me back to the Carlson family.

Having read this far into the book (assuming you haven't skipped forward to the Epilogue!), you now know quite a lot about my life. So, I'll keep the following description of the events that led up to you holding this book in your hands as brief as possible.

Healing from my childhood began in earnest in my mid-thirties after my first experience with Reiki. Soon after that, in 2006, I relocated to the USA with James and my young children.

Over the years that followed, I continued healing from my deep-seated emotional wounds by working with various healers and becoming certified in numerous energy healing modalities, along with NLP.

As mentioned earlier in the book, during an Akashic Record mentorship in 2012, my Akashic team conveyed that I would write several books in my life. Despite my enthusiasm and initial attempts to channel the information, it didn't flow as easily as expected. Over time, I realized that the delay in writing wasn't about my readiness for the information, but rather my own need to grow, experience life, and face the fears that were blocking me. Now, as I complete this first book, I see how those years of waiting have been crucial to the unfolding of this writing journey, where everything came together in a fluid, easy way.

In 2019, while on retreat with my beloved spiritual teacher, Gangaji, I had the privilege of speaking with her in a small group. There were only five of us in the room that day, and she spoke with each of us in turn. I don't recall her exact words to me, but the gist of it was that she was looking forward to seeing how this transmission of *Love* I had received would take form in the world. As she spoke, her eyes were ablaze with *Love*. I felt a call to action of some kind, but nothing really kicked off afterward.

In 2022, my energetic guides encouraged me to start writing again. The words flowed easily, making the process both cathartic and enjoyable. I wasn't sure what form it would take, but I continued writing without needing to know the outcome.

Then, my dad died suddenly in November 2022. After the intense, overwhelming, and incapacitating grief, anger, and sadness had subsided somewhat, I discovered that something profound had changed inside of me. I emerged like a butterfly from a chrysalis with a strong desire to write my book and get moving. It felt unstoppable.

A few months later, I received an email blast from the Gangaji Foundation with news that Gangaji would be interviewed in an upcoming telesummit. It was unusual for her to take part in these events, so I took notice, and keen to hear her speak, I signed up.

I don't know about you, but telesummit fatigue sets in quickly with me! So much so that I've since given them up. I find them both depleting and exhausting. With so many speakers each day, running for several days, I get over-saturated and give up listening. Gangaji was on day five. I never made it that far! I'd lost the will to go on at that point! Anyway, the important thing to note is that indirectly she was the catalyst that led me to participate in that event. I wouldn't have heard about it or signed up otherwise.

At the beginning of the telesummit, I heard a pair of life coaches being interviewed. Something about their energy caught my attention. I felt strongly drawn to them for some reason, so I signed up for a telesummit they were hosting. Yes, a sucker for punishment, I know!

Here comes the magic. In that telesummit, one of the speakers was Kristine Carlson, Richard Carlson's wife. With great sadness, I learned that he had died in 2006. I thoroughly enjoyed listening to Kristine speak and felt we were meant to be connected. She shared about the books she has written and published and about an online course she runs with a highly acclaimed editor, Debra Evans, called the Book Doulas' Incubator Program.

Immediately after the interview, I jumped onto the Book Doulas' website to find out more about the course.

I was very nervous as I read about it, primarily because I didn't regard myself as a writer back then. There was a fair amount of imposter syndrome flaring up. No one had read any of my work, and I was concerned that the other participants would be superior writers to me. Nevertheless, I signed up because I knew I was meant to experience their offerings and receive their wisdom.

I benefited in many wonderful ways from working with Kristine and Debra. I loved being part of the Incubator course. And as the months passed, I became confident about my writing abilities. It was such a positive, empowering experience that I signed up for their next level, the Momentum program, and had several private sessions with them, focusing on my book.

In all likelihood, you would not be reading this book if I hadn't come across Kristine and Debra. Between them, they encouraged and guided me to the extent that I knew I could turn my writing endeavors into a real book — one that I would be proud to share with the world.

So here I am, sitting at my desk in the living room, watching the birds eagerly making nests on my front porch, and finishing off my book, preparing it for the next phase of its creation process before publication.

Along with some beautiful synchronicities, Divine timing was undoubtedly at play here. I suspect that no amount of forcing or pushing would have speeded up my healing process or the timing of the writing of this book. The truth is we have no control over Divine timing.

While this can be frustrating at times, it offers a wonderful opportunity to trust that a force much greater than ourselves — the beloved Divine — has a plan for our lives. We simply need to take the actions that our inner guidance brings to our attention and trust the process. The Divine tends to only reveal one step at a time and gives us no clue where we are heading or when.

It's so perfect to me that Gangaji was the one who led me to Kristine Carlson, albeit in a roundabout way. Clearly, I needed a gentle nudge from the Universe in the right direction!

I love the full-circle element of these events. From when my twenty-seven-year-old self was drawn to Richard Carlson's self-help book, all the way up to becoming a published author in my fifties — with Kristine Carlson having played a critical role in helping me bring this book to you. One self-help book to another!

Through my various adventures, I've shed countless layers of suffering from my past and genuinely opened into loving myself unconditionally. And I'm here to let you know that you can do the same.

In writing *Droplets of Love*, my heartfelt intention has always been that it might encourage, inspire, or reassure others, particularly those who are brave enough to make changes in their lives, ready to heal from traumatic events, and prepared to take a blind leap of faith into loving themselves.

I urge you to be patient in your healing process and surrender to the flow of life, to what the Divine has planned for you. Trust, trust, trust.

Regardless of your background or where your life goes

from this moment forward, I'm here with you every step of the way. You've got this!

Most importantly, always remember that you are a droplet of *Love*, an aspect of the Divine.

# Transformational
# Resources

# SERENITY GEMS

## A QUICK GUIDE TO CALM & RECENTER YOURSELF

Feeling triggered emotionally? It's okay — it happens to us all sometimes. When emotions, thoughts, or memories are stirred up, regard it as an opportunity to heal. Be gentle with yourself and know that inner growth tends to come from facing life's challenges. Here are some fast, effective ways to reinstate calm and recenter yourself when you're feeling triggered.

*Remember:* Although this often seems highly improbable to our analytical mind, emotions and thoughts are not personal. They are simply energy that wishes to move through us. Do your best to welcome them without judgment.

You'll find a downloadable pdf version of "Serenity Gems" at: **www.rachellinnett.com/serenity-gems.**

## BREATHING TIPS

Deep breathing is a rapid, effective way to promote relaxation.

◆ Begin with some slow, full breaths. Inhale deeply through your nose and exhale through your mouth.

◆ After a few minutes, continue your slow, gentle pace and add in belly breathing. Direct the air to fill your belly, placing your hands on your abdomen to feel it rise and fall.

◆ For even deeper relaxation, transition to the 4:8 breathing pattern: inhale for a count of 4, and exhale for a count of 8, so the exhalation is twice as long as the inhalation. Continue for 5 to 10 minutes to enhance calm.

## LOOK UPWARD FOR INSTANT CALM

When emotions run high, your eyes tend to look down. Instead, gently shift your gaze upward without moving your head. This simple action helps calm your brain and reduces emotional intensity, helping you feel more balanced and centered.

How to do it:

◆ Focus on a spot above eye level.

◆ Hold your gaze upward for 20 to 30 seconds.

◆ Notice the shift in how you feel.

◆ Use this technique whenever you feel overwhelmed to quickly shift your emotional state and access a sense of calm and clarity.

## STIMULATE THE VAGUS NERVE

This is a gentle way to activate your body's natural relaxation response and calm your nervous system.

- Use your fingertips to gently tap or massage the area behind your earlobe (the mastoid bone) on both sides of your head.

- Continue tapping or massaging for 30 seconds to 1 minute.

- Focusing on deep belly breathing as you do this further deepens the effect.

## AIRTIGHT CONTAINER

Visualize the specific triggering situation in your mind. If it appears in color, change it to black and white. Freeze it like a paused video and make the image as small as possible. With gentleness and kindness, pop it in an imaginary airtight container. Add any energetic cords connecting you to the situation. Then, move the container away from you to a distance where you feel safe and relaxed. If it feels right for you, you can give the container to the Divine for resolution and transmutation back to Source energy.

## QUICK MOOD CHANGERS

Shake your body, dance, exercise, hum, sing, or take a shower or a warm Epsom salt bath. Spend time in nature by going for a walk. Any of these will help shift the energy.

## SELF-CARE

Let any tears fall if they arise, be gentle with yourself, eat nourishing food, avoid alcohol, and rest well. Allow time for quiet reflection, and refuse to believe negative stories about the past or future. Remember emotions are just energy. Think of a few things that you are grateful for, however big or small.

## TAKE TIME TO PROCESS

Most likely the steps described above will have created a sense of relaxation, inner peace, and spaciousness in you. Soak this sensation into every level of your being. Enjoy it to the full. Then, when you are ready, I highly recommend addressing those troublesome emotions and thoughts. Rather than brushing them under the rug, give them your attention. In the long term, this will boost your healing process.

- In a quiet space, when you won't be interrupted, invite the emotions or situation into your mind's eye. Breathe into them, welcoming whatever arises: anger, grief, sadness, self-hatred, loneliness, frustration. Breathe deeply into the core of whatever feelings you are experiencing.

- Even if it gets very intense, or physical sensations show up, gently bring your awareness back to breathing calm and a sense of spaciousness into the emotions, breathing out whatever is ready to leave.

- If resistance appears, welcome that too, and breathe into it. Gently let that resistant part of you know it's safe to experience and release these feelings.

## ADDITIONAL SUPPORT

◆ Beyond this guide, consider using the other tools discussed in this book to assist you on your healing journey.

◆ Remember you're not alone on this courageous path of inner healing. I'm here, offering support and tools for your transformational journey. Be patient, take good care of yourself, and trust your inner wisdom. Always remember, you are the expert on you.

Check out my website **www.rachellinnett.com** for additional *Droplets of Love* resources.

Keep these simple steps handy to quickly regain calm and clarity whenever you feel triggered.

Always remember that every challenge is an opportunity for growth.

You've got this!

# ALCHEMY TOOLS

## EASY TOOLS TO HELP YOU MAKE BRILLIANT DECISIONS

In Chapter 4, I suggested that you could employ some techniques to help you make decisions in alignment with your deeper self. That might involve determining which modality, healing practitioner, doctor, or treatment plan, is a good fit for you. You can also use these approaches to assist you in making all kinds of other decisions: whether to accept an invitation, where to go on holiday, what to order from a menu, which brand of supplement to buy, or which route to take home.

They all involve checking in with our inner guidance, which enables us to navigate our lives with more ease and harmony. Our body never lies. It is a truth teller. So, when we tune in to our body's sensations, listening to its cues, and taking action based on what it's showing us, we find ourselves being steered towards situations and people that will be beneficial for us — and away from the ones that aren't such a good fit. In this way, we can stay in our sovereign selves, trusting how we feel, rather than automatically following what others say we should do.

You'll recall that earlier in this book I described a quick and easy way to tap into the physical sensations inside your body when you are looking to determine if particular situations or relationships are in alignment with your True

Self. See what your body says to you when you bring to mind a specific choice. What signals does it relay to you? The beauty of this approach is that it's discreet; no-one else will know what you're up to when you consult your inner guidance!

Below I'm sharing with you three additional approaches that I use regularly. You can use the first one surreptitiously while you're out and about, but the other two are best suited for quiet moments when you can go inward and have some undisturbed time to yourself. Have a play around with them and discover which of them work well for you and feel easy to use.

## BODY PENDULUM

Take some deep breaths. Breathe in the qualities of spaciousness and calm, and exhale any tension residing in your body. Continue for a few minutes.

Stand up with your feet hip distance apart, arms loose at your sides.

Begin by identifying what your specific positive and negative responses are. Close your eyes and ask your body to show you what your "yes" is. Give yourself a few moments, keep breathing deeply and your body will show you.

Then clear your internal screen in your mind's eye before asking your body what its "no" is.

Most people find their body leans forward slightly for their "yes", and then sways backward for their "no." But others have the opposite response: Their bodies go backward for "yes" and forward for "no."

I suggest that you test it a few times, building your confidence in the process, by asking a few questions that you know the answer to. Like, "Is my name (e.g., Rachel)?"

Once you know how your body moves, you don't need to go through that part again. It tends to stay the same. It's a good idea to recheck periodically though.

Before you ask a question, clear your mind, and let go of attachment to outcome. Be patient with yourself because letting go of any attachment can take some practice! For this reason, I often ask each question three times.

Bring to mind a decision you need to make, and ask something along the lines of "Will (this treatment or energy healing modality, etc.) be beneficial for (this ailment or situation)?" or "Is (name of a practitioner or therapist) a good fit for me?" Then wait to see how your body responds. Does your body move to your "yes" or "no" position?

If you're going to ask another question, always remember to clear the screen internally after you've received your response. Gently shaking your body can help to reset your body in preparation for the next question.

## BODY SCALES

This approach is great when you have two options you're considering.

Take some slow, deep, full breaths, exhaling any stress, tension, or worry. Shake your arms gently to release energy and relax your muscles.

Stand up, with arms bent in front of you at right angles and palms facing the sky, as if you were holding a tray. Simply imagine one of your options on the palm of one hand.

Make it as vivid as you can. Maybe you sense it energetically, or perhaps you have an image of it, or feel or hear it in some way. Then turn your attention to your other hand and place the alternative option on that palm. As for the other option, make it as real as possible, in whatever way comes to you naturally.

Do your very best to let go of any attachment to the outcome; stay neutral.

With one option on each palm, ask yourself a pertinent question, such as: "Which one is in alignment with my highest good?;" or "Which one will create the best results?;" or "Which one will help me the most?" To minimize confusion and ensure a reliable response, make sure to ask only one question at a time. Then wait to see what happens. Breathe deeply and relax. You'll likely find one palm rises up, perhaps a little, or maybe more dramatically, and the other palm lowers to some degree.

The best option for you will be on the raised hand. If your hands remain at the same level, it probably means that either option would be fine.

## INTO THE WOODS

This is an excellent tool for more than one option. Although I'd keep the number of choices relatively small to ensure that you're getting clear and accurate responses.

Take some deep breaths, exhale stress, tension, or any worry, and let yourself relax.

In your mind's eye, imagine you're walking along a path

through some woods, and you come to a place where the path splits into alternative routes. There is a path for each of your options. Place a different option of what you are considering on each path. This could relate to anything at all, e.g., choice of career, which home to rent, where to go on vacation, or which doctor, therapist, or healer to work with.

Then travel down the first path. Pay close attention to how you feel and what the sensations are in your body. Also pay attention to any tightness or constriction, expansiveness, or lightheartedness. Perhaps thoughts and images will appear. Can you hear any words of insight or guidance, or do you have a sense of knowing? What do you sense as you progress along the path?

Then look at your energetic response in the future. Take yourself out on the timeline by six months, and check in with your body; then project ahead a year, followed by five years into the future, or whatever future point feels most appropriate for you. For future reference, it can be helpful to make notes on what you experience.

Then clear the screen in your mind, and repeat for the other options, one at a time.

Your body will provide you with valuable and reliable feedback on each option to help you to make a sound decision. Sometimes we discover that in the shorter term, something might be fine, but in the longer term, it might not end up being the best way forward for you.

# GOLDEN NUGGETS

Here are some details on how you can benefit from my various offerings as you navigate your spiritual and healing path. I'm excited to partner with you in meaningful ways as you transform your life in beautiful, empowering ways. May you find something valuable or useful within this section.

## NEWSLETTER

Stay connected and be the first to hear about my latest offerings designed to support lasting change. Join a community of like-minded individuals dedicated to personal growth and transformation. To sign up, please visit my website: **www.rachellinnett.com/join-my-mailing-list.**

## YOUTUBE CHANNEL

I invite you to explore my YouTube channel, where I share free videos designed to support your spiritual growth and personal transformation. Whether you're looking for guided meditations, energy work, or spiritual insights, you'll find content created with *Love* and intention. It's a great way to connect more deeply with the work I do, and I hope it offers inspiration and healing for your journey. You can check out my videos here:
**www.youtube.com/@RachelJaneLinnett.**

## GROUP EVENTS

To find out more about current group events, please visit my website at **www. rachellinnett.com**.

## PRIVATE MENTORSHIP/COACHING PROGRAMS

I mentor and coach individuals who are deeply committed to their personal growth and spiritual evolution. Working 1:1 with me creates a space for profound transformation, clearing away deep-rooted energetic blocks that have held you back. As we work together, you'll be guided to connect with your True Self, raise your vibration, increase your capacity to love yourself unconditionally, and create a joyful, fulfilling life. My clients experience significant, lasting shifts that empower them to live more authentically, confidently, and with greater purpose.

If you're ready to take the next step in your transformation and align with your highest potential, I'm right here to support you in making those shifts a reality.

Visit my website — **www.rachellinnett.com** — to book a free Discovery Call, and let's explore how I can best support you on your journey.

## GUIDED MEDITATIONS

In my website store at **www.rachellinnett.com**, you'll find a selection of potent meditations to help you deeply relax, calm your nervous system, and connect with your body's innate healing energy. Created to foster profound shifts in self-love, balance, and inner peace, they're a powerful resource for anyone looking to enrich their healing and spiritual journey. Let *Love* take the lead and experience how these meditations can support your transformation.

## MY ARTWORK WEBSITE

Here you'll find a selection of the beauty I love to create. I'll never tire of seeing what emerges from a blank canvas! **www.rachelspaintings.art**

## OTHER RESOURCES TO SUPPORT YOU

I have some additional golden nuggets for you, including Gangaji's website information, along with a selection of transformational tools and practitioners that I highly recommend. I also have a few great book recommendations and links to some of my current favorite things that I find tremendously valuable to me on my healing journey.

To ensure that their website links are up to date, and that you're kept up to speed with my latest gems, I'm directing you to a resources page on my website: **www.rachellinnett.com/golden-nuggets.**

# Acknowledgements

# ACKNOWLEDGEMENTS

Where do I start, James? Perhaps with eternal gratitude for your dedication and hard work over the years as you provided for our family. Your support gave me the freedom to focus on healing from my childhood and diving into the world of transformational change. As I've been writing this book, you've kept me sane and helped me regain my sense of humor when the going got tough. Thank you for believing in me and for pushing me beyond where I thought I could go. Beyond that, your stellar support with technology-related matters deserves a medal — especially because, as we both know, I have an uncanny ability to cause unexpected and inexplicable effects on electrical items! Lastly, thank you for picking up all those domestic duties while I spent long hours in my studio, writing and fine-tuning my manuscript. You are my love, and I'm immensely grateful, in countless ways, for the life we've shared since bonding over hydraulics homework at Newcastle University.

To my gorgeous Jess and Josh: Thank you from the core of my being for choosing me as your mum, accepting me just as I am, and embracing my quirky, non-traditional ways. I love you to the moon and back a zillion times. Your ongoing support and encouragement in all my endeavors fill me with joy and make my heart swell with love. Jess, your beautiful photography captured me in ways I didn't think possible — you're incredibly talented — and your exceptional creativity never fails to inspire me. Josh, your humor is a gift to everyone you meet, and your calming presence soothes my soul. I'm so grateful for both of you.

Over the past few years, I have been fortunate to cross paths with five incredible, compassionate, and supportive healers: Sarah Rotella, Deb Gottlieb, Gregor Bertram, Sharon Sklar, and Catherine Collins. Each of you has played an invaluable role in my healing journey, offering powerful support when life got overly intense — especially during the writing of this book. I am profoundly grateful for your patience in listening to my endless verbal processing, your wisdom and expertise that continue to inspire me, and the laughter you've brought into my life. From the depths of my heart, thank you for walking this path with me.

Writing this book has been a rollercoaster ride. At times, I was in the flow and loving it, but there were plenty of moments when I struggled, as if wading through treacle, while navigating some exceedingly tough challenges. I'm deeply grateful for all the love and support I received from dear friends as this book was being breathed into life. A special thank you goes out to Maggie, Fiona, Cyndi, and Judith. In those hardest times, you were there — patiently listening to my frustrations, cheering me on, and offering words that truly energized me. I'm deeply grateful for your insights and for laughing with me at the absurd twists and turns. Thank you, beautiful soul sisters.

It's hard to put into words how profoundly grateful I am to Gangaji, my spiritual touchstone. My life was turned upside down and inside out when I first read your books and attended your retreats. Over the last fourteen years of being your student, I've peeled away countless layers of conditioning and gradually revealed more of my True Self. Your presence in my life opened my heart and allowed *Love* to lead the way. I'm deeply honored that you graciously wrote a review of this book. Your words will help expand the reach of this transformational work, of which, it turns out, I am a loving custodian. Thank you for encouraging me to find my own unique way of expressing *Love* in the world.

I am eternally grateful to my Akashic connections and my energetic guides — my perpetual companions, come rain or shine. Thank you for guiding me on my spiritual path, for the endless insights, and for nudging me to act when I'd really rather not. As my trust in your presence and impact on my life grew, so did my courage to dive headfirst into challenging situations, rather than avoid them. Every single time, even when it's highly uncomfortable or painful, you lead me in a direction that deepens my realization of knowing myself as *Love*. Together, we've been an unstoppable force in bringing *Droplets of Love* to life. Thank you for always being by my side.

The day I heard Kristine Carlson being interviewed on a webinar in early 2023, something inside me knew my life was about to change. Signing up for The Book Incubator, led by Kristine and Debra Evans, was undoubtedly a monumental catalyst in the creation of this book. Thank you both for teaching me so much about writing and publishing. It was truly nerve-wracking the first time I volunteered to read my work out to the class, doubtful of how my writing or voice would be received. Yet, every step of the way, your insightful feedback guided me to improve my writing, dig deeper, aim higher, and, most importantly, you boosted my confidence. Without you, this book would not have made it into print. Of that, I am certain.

Megan Williams and Ira Vergani at TSPA — oh my! I have been blown away by the TSPA experience. Thank you for your superb guidance, wisdom, and boundless humor throughout the creation of this book. You were both incredible at responding in calm, practical ways when challenges arose, reassuring me that everything would work out. Whether smoothing bumps or celebrating highs, you always had my back. Your belief in this project and your encouragement made all the difference in seeing it through. I'm so grateful for your patience when I needed extra time to finish my manuscript and for your unwavering support every step of the way.

A massive thank you to Tracy Hetherington for your beautiful graphics work. I loved how you jumped right into the mix with my design ideas and teamed up with me so effortlessly to create such a gorgeous front cover. As a fellow artist, I know how challenging it can be to collaborate with other creatives, but you seemed to read my mind and made the entire design process feel easy and fun.

For coming to the rescue at the last minute when I was in a tight spot, Kathie Lynas, as my wonderful editor, you brought this book over the finish line with strength, grace, and humor. I knew I was in good hands from the moment we first spoke. When I asked if reading the book had triggered you — screening for objectivity — you laughed and reassured me that it hadn't. Thank you for your smart, wise editorial suggestions, and most importantly, for preserving my voice. It was truly a pleasure working with you.

Donna Cravotta, your boundless enthusiasm and creative energy have joyfully guided me through the marketing and PR journey for *Droplets of Love*. Your ideas, insights, and expertise have been instrumental in shaping a plan to bring this book to those who need it most. Thank you for making this process both fun and exciting, and for helping me stay grounded and focused as we worked together to share this message with the world. I couldn't have done it without you.

As I bring this to a close, I am deeply grateful for everything that has happened in my life that has brought me to the point where this book was ready to be birthed. To my family of origin: Without the experiences we shared, I wouldn't be in a position to assist others on their healing journeys from traumatic childhoods. To the multitude of people who have supported and cheered me on along the way — whether I mentioned you here or not — your enthusiasm and encouragement have meant the world to me. Thank you, from the bottom of my heart, for celebrating this creation with me. I love you, and I honor you.

Onwards!

# ABOUT RACHEL

Rachel Linnett, a transformational coach, spiritual mentor and artist with over 18 years of experience, guides others on journeys of self-healing and inner discovery. Originally from England and now living by the ocean in Connecticut, Rachel's own path of healing from a challenging childhood inspired her insatiable passion for empowering others to do the same. A creative soul with a love for painting, color, and flowers, she infuses her work with warmth, humor, and deep insight. By helping clients connect with their inner wisdom, Rachel supports them in embracing lives aligned with their True Selves — filled with authenticity, purpose, and joy.

Check out her websites at:
**www.rachellinnett.com**
**www.rachelspaintings.art**